Turn Yourselves and Live

Rod W. Jeppsen

Ezekiel 18:32

Is Any Thing Too Hard for the Lord?

Genesis 18:14

Turn Yourselves and Live
Is Any Thing Too Hard for the Lord?

VESCORP
9500 South 500 West, Suite 209
Sandy, UT 84070

Call 801-255-4010 for the bookstore nearest you.

Library of Congress Catalog Card Number
97-91254
ISBN 0-9661898-0-9

First Printing: March 1998
Second Printing: January 2001

10 9 8 7 6 5 4 3 2

Cover design: Eric Richards

Dedication

This book is dedicated
to all individuals who have struggled
with a compulsive sexual behavior.

Acknowledgments

I did not prepare this book without help.
As I shared my ideas about this book
with my friends and asked them to contribute,
they overwhelmingly agreed.
To these, some of my closest friends,

I say thank you!

Table of Contents

Preface . . . . *vii*
Introduction *1*

It's My Problem
Chapter 1 . . . .*24*

The Healing Begins with Christ
Chapter 2 . . . .*29*

Humility—The Foundation
of Repentance
Chapter 3 . . . .*33*

Developing Christ-centered
Rational Thoughts
Chapter 4 . . . .*43*

The Root of the Problem
Chapter 5 . . . .*70*

Surrendering Negative Emotions
to Heavenly Father
Chapter 6 . . . .*98*

Using Divine Relationships
to Fill Emotional Needs
Chapter 7 . . . .*108*

Christ Has the Power
to Heal Our Weaknesses
Chapter 8 . . . .*130*

Prepare Every Needful Thing
Chapter 9 . . . .*139*

We Believe All Things
Chapter 10 . . . .*142*

Index *161*

Preface

How did I get interested in this topic? My parents were good parents, but we didn't talk about sex. In my home very little was said about our bodies or how babies are created or how they come to this earth. Knowing my grandparents, they probably didn't say *anything* to my parents about sex. When the subject of sex education came up with some of my adult friends, I learned that they came from similar backgrounds. Sex just wasn't discussed a generation or two ago. As a result, everything I learned about sex came from TV, radio, movies, or my friends at school; consequently much of it was not accurate or helpful.

Early in my marriage, I sought out a counselor to help me deal with the improper attitudes and feelings I had learned during my teenage years.

Meeting with a counselor who had a strong testimony of the gospel and was well respected in his profession was very healing and worthwhile. The counselor charged forty dollars per hour. I thought at that rate I would be cured in no time. But it wasn't that easy—even though I was, at the same time, reading self-improvement books and gathering scriptures that seemed applicable to compulsive behaviors.

This book is the result of my own struggle and recovery as well as the experiences of people I met through a support group and people I worked with over the years in my church leadership positions. As I have held interviews and listened closely to numerous individuals who have chosen compulsive sexual behaviors, I have been able to identify many irrational thinking patterns and emotional out-of-balance behaviors that get people into this compulsive behavior. I also learned many ways individuals can deal with emotions and feelings in a positive way to get them *out* of the compulsive behavior. *The most important thing I learned about helping people overcome this compulsive behavior is that any successful plan for recovery needs to be Christ-centered.* We become victorious only as we surrender our weaknesses to Christ and become one with Him. As we turn to Christ, we begin the inner healing. Every temptation can be overcome with faith on the Lord Jesus Christ.

Speaking to his son Helaman, Alma said, *"Preach unto them repentance, and faith on the Lord Jesus Christ; teach them to humble themselves and to be meek and lowly in heart; teach them to withstand every temptation of the devil, with their faith on the Lord Jesus Christ."* (Alma 37:33)

This book is unique because it is a workbook that allows you to work through your feelings. As you record your feelings and begin to take responsibility for them, you will see progress (although at times it may be slow) in overcoming what I have come to call a "drug of choice"— a compulsive sexual lifestyle.

The title of this book explains a two-fold program for surrender and recovery. The first part is to turn toward Christ and surrender your compulsive sexual behavior. As you do your part, Christ will do His part—His power, strength, and peace will be with you and the actual healing will occur.

Elder Boyd K. Packer said, "It is contrary to the order of heaven for any soul to be locked into compulsive, immoral behavior with no way out!" (*Ensign*, November 1986, p. 18)

The Savior said: *"Continue to minister; for ye know not but what they will return and repent, and come unto me with full purpose of heart, and I shall heal them."* (3 Nephi 18:32) He also said, *"Will ye not now return unto me, and repent of your sins, and be converted, that I may heal you?"* (3 Nephi 9:13)

This book is designed to teach you the steps to take and the tools to do spiritual surgery rather than give you a spiritual Band-Aid®. A Band-Aid® only covers up the wound and may come off after a few days. Spiritual surgery may be painful, but it is necessary in order for lasting emotional and spiritual healing to occur. To accept spiritual surgery is to draw on the power of Christ. Only with Christ's help can consistent progress and healing take place. Christ is a solid foundation: *"And now, my sons, remember, remember that it is upon the rock of our Redeemer, who is Christ, the Son of God, that ye must build your foundation; that when the devil shall send forth his mighty winds, yea, his shafts in the whirlwind, yea, when all his hail and his mighty storm shall beat upon you, it shall have no power over you to drag you down to the gulf of misery and endless wo, because of the rock*

upon which ye are built, which is a sure foundation, a founda-
tion whereon if men build they cannot fall." (Helaman 5:12)

The personal histories of compulsive individuals in the book are true; however, some names and situations have been changed to protect those involved. The people I mention are all real people who are productive citizens. By all outward appearances they seem "normal." They succeeded in turning their lives around; they are becoming their best selves through the power of the Atonement and their relationship with Jesus Christ. By surrendering their weaknesses to Christ, they each achieved victory.

The ten-step program for recovery contained in this book is based on the experiences, setbacks, moments of success, and eventual recovery of these individuals and others who have now chosen a Christ-centered life.

I do not consider myself an expert on this subject. However, I do know what has worked for many individuals, including myself, and I do know that any successful plan for recovery must be Christ-centered. I also know we are sent to earth to learn, grow, and develop a personal relationship with the Savior.

I'm very confident that as you use this ten-step program, you will make progress in surrendering your compulsive sexual behavior and building a Christ-centered life. You can achieve the results the Savior promised when He said, *"Peace I leave with you, my peace I give unto you: not as the world giveth, give I unto you. Let not your heart be troubled, neither let it be afraid."* (John 14:27)

ntroduction

I wanted to stop, but I didn't know how. I tried everything to quit. I told myself so often that this would be the last time, and I would never do it again! But I did it again and again. Each time I did it, I felt guilty, depressed, and irritable. I felt like a loser. Each time it happened, I thought, "Why am I the only one who has to deal with this problem?" Everyone else seemed normal except me.

I couldn't bring myself to tell anyone about my problem. I was so embarrassed. I had been able to accomplish just about everything I put my mind to—except this. I've tried so hard to stop and it just keeps happening.

I've tried everything I can think of and if something does seem to help, my progress is short-term and then I fall again. Last week I promised that I would never do it again. And now, a week later, I have already broken my commitment.

Do these thoughts sound familiar? Have you had similar thoughts or know of someone who has? These are thoughts of despair and a call for help. The title of this book is *Turn Yourselves and Live*. *Is Any Thing Too Hard for the Lord?* Recovery is a joint effort between you and the Lord. As you strive to do your best, the Lord will make up the difference. He will replace fear, doubt, and despair with peace, faith, and hope.

THE PARABLE OF THE LAMB

There was once a little lamb born into a very good flock. The lamb was pure and innocent. As he grew older, there came a time when the other lambs teased him and none of them wanted to play with him. The lamb felt rejected and lonely and not even his parents seemed to understand. One day he got into a fight with them and concluded that his parents didn't love him. Feeling totally rejected, he began to feel very sorry for himself. His self-pity turned to anger and he decided to leave the flock.

The lamb walked alone for awhile; then another lamb happened by.

He didn't know him very well, but they soon found out they had a lot in common. At last he had someone to talk with who would understand his story of self-pity.

The Grain Bin

After listening for about an hour, the friend said, "I know where the farmer keeps his grain. Let's go to his grain bin. It will help you feel better. It always works for me."

To get to the farmer's bin, the lamb had to leave the pasture—something he had been taught by his parents never to do. The lamb said to himself, "It's not my fault I'm leaving the pasture. It's my parents' fault. They are making me leave because of the way they treated me." Keeping that thought in mind, he kneeled down, squeezed through the small hole in the fence and began to explore the pasture next door with his new friend.

The grass was much greener there and everything seemed more enticing. The lamb was so excited he didn't notice any of the ant beds or the snakes that slithered through the new pasture. Since he had been troubled with ants and snakes in the old pasture, this new pasture seemed better.

While in the pasture, he could forget his feelings of rejection, self-pity, and anger. He felt alive. There were many new things that attracted him. He said, "This is what I've been looking for. This is the answer to my problems."

His friend led him to the grain bin behind the farmer's barn. The grain tasted delicious. How could something that tasted so good and made him feel so alive be bad for him?

That night he went back to his own pasture. His old feelings of rejection, self-pity, and anger were still with him. In addition, he now felt guilty for going into the forbidden pasture and eating the grain because the lamb knew that, while there is a time and place for grain, the amounts had to be carefully limited. Grain was not part of a young lamb's normal diet and if he ate too much grain, it could even cause his death. His feelings of guilt stayed with him for several days. He couldn't shake them. He knew what he had done was not right. As he tried to forget the guilt, he started daydreaming about the farmer's grain bin. Whenever he was thinking about the grain bin, he didn't feel guilty. Fantasizing about the grain bin soon was not enough; he returned to the grain bin—this time without his friend. While his head was in the grain bin, he felt like a new person, and for the moment he forgot his guilt, rejection, and self-pity. On the way home, though, he felt even more guilty and depressed.

The lamb wanted to escape feeling rejected, lonely, angry, and hurt; but all his old problems were still with him. He soon learned that he could forget them only when he was at the grain bin, so it became very difficult for him to leave it alone. The grain bin—which he thought was the answer to his problems—soon became his biggest problem. Too much grain doesn't digest quickly enough and could ferment in his stomach creating gas—enough to kill him. Even full-grown sheep can die from an overdose of grain. The lamb had already experienced serious discomfort from the grain; he knew he must stop going to the grain bin.

Often the lamb would stand right next to the fence and say, "I'm not going to the grain bin. No, I'm not going to the grain bin. I'm just standing here." After standing for about ten minutes the lamb would say, "I'm not going to the other pasture, I'm just going to see if I still fit inside the hole in the fence, but I'm not going to the other pasture." He would slide part way through the hole in the fence; then he would go all the way through the fence and stand on the other side and say, "I'm not going to the farmer's barn. I'm just standing here, but I'm not going to the farmer's barn." After standing for a few minutes, the lamb would say, "I'm going down to the barn just to see if the farmer parked his tractor behind the barn, but I'm not going to the grain bin." The lamb would go to the farmer's barn and sure enough the tractor would be parked behind the barn right next to the grain bin.

The lamb would finally say, "Since I've come this far, I'll just take one spoonful of grain and then leave." After one spoonful, the lamb would say, "I've gone this far, what difference does it make now how much I eat?" Then the lamb would eat and eat until he felt sick.

On the way home, he would be filled with depression and guilt once more. He had told himself this would never ever happen again. Each time he went to the grain bin he promised himself he would never return. But he went back again and again.

The Grain Bin is a Compulsive Sexual Lifestyle

In this story the grain bin is compared to _____ (Use this blank to write in the compulsive sexual behavior you're trying to stop. You may want to abbreviate or put a code word for the behavior to keep it confidential.)

At first someone may have introduced you to it, or you may have just discovered it on your own. It doesn't matter how you got started; with Christ's help you can surrender the compulsive behavior. This book will teach you the steps to take and the tools to use to turn yourself to Christ so you won't keep going to the grain bin. As we turn to Christ, we begin to live.

You cannot overcome your compulsive sexual behavior by yourself. You need the help of Heavenly Father and the Savior. *We were not sent to earth to see how much we could do by ourselves, but rather, to see how much we could do with*

God's help. With total surrender to God's help you will have success.

THE COMPULSIVE BEHAVIOR PATTERN
Any compulsive behavior has the following pattern:

> First, we learn the behavior.
> Second, we use it to cover up unresolved feelings and out-of-balance emotions.
> Third, we deny that the behavior is a problem.
> Fourth, we never tell anyone about it (isolation).
> Fifth, we turn to the behavior again and again.

Let's analyze this pattern in the Parable of the Lamb:

First, the lamb learned the behavior.
- He was feeling lonely. He went with a "friend" that he didn't know well.
- His "friend" introduced him to the grain bin.

Second, he used the pleasure of the trip to the grain bin to cover up unresolved feelings and out-of-balance emotions.
- The lamb chose to leave instead of resolving his angry feelings with his parents.
- He allowed his feelings of rejection to turn into self-pity.

Third, he denied that his behavior was a problem and put the blame elsewhere; he was not ready to admit that he was responsible for the problem.

- The lamb rationalized that it was okay to go to the other pasture since he was upset at his parents, even though he had been taught not to leave his own pasture.

Fourth, he never told anyone about it (isolation).
- He rationalized that he would never do it again and since he was not going to do it again, he didn't have to tell anyone or do anything about it.
- After he went to the pasture, he did not go home and discuss it with his parents or another trusted individual. He kept his behavior a big secret.

Fifth, he repeated the behavior again and again.
- He stood by the fence of temptation and kept telling himself he would never cross it.
- The lamb used each slip-up—each step toward the grain bin—to justify the next, and kept moving closer and closer until he finally went all the way to the bin again.

This is the cycle of a compulsive behavior. To get out of this compulsive behavior, a person needs to begin the following process.

SURRENDER THE WEAKNESS TO CHRIST AND BEGIN A CHRIST-CENTERED LIFE.

You can lay the foundation for a Christ-centered life in the following ways:

First, recognize your need for help to stop your compulsive behavior.

Second, seek out a trusted friend, counselor, bishop— someone who has the ability and resources to help.

Most of us who get caught up in compulsive behaviors eventually hit rock bottom. The grain bin stops working as a means of covering up our painful feelings and becomes the main problem. The only way out is to humble ourselves, talk to a trusted friend, and determine to live a Christ-centered life. Spiritual growth begins on bended knees of humility.

The Drug of Lust

A person chooses a compulsive sexual behavior in an attempt to drown or cover out-of-balance emotions. Over several years, I worked with many individuals who had chosen a compulsive sexual lifestyle as an attempt to deal with feelings and emotions that they didn't want to feel. They literally used compulsive sexual behavior as a drug to cover up the pain caused by some feeling. Lust became their drug of choice.

Let's analyze this pattern. When a sexually compulsive person is emotionally out-of-balance, he chooses lust to cover up his emotions instead of using these emotions to turn to God. At first the god of lust seems to provide all the answers. It seems to be an easy way to feel good. It produces excitement and an emotional high; but after the fix of lust has been injected into the body, the person cannot avoid the side effects.

There are always side effects when people drink alcohol, smoke tobacco, or do drugs. There are also side effects from the drug of lust. One of the real side effects of _____ (write in your sexual compulsive behavior) is the ever-increasing desire to lust. Lust can literally become a drug of choice. Lust then becomes the primary problem—because lust can never be satisfied. Enough is never enough. Lust wears many faces—inappropriate thoughts, masturbation, pornography, heterosexual relationships, homosexuality, lesbianism, prostitution, exhibitionism, voyeurism, child molestation, incest, etc. Lust has no boundaries. Lust prevents a person from becoming his best self, because it allows the natural man to take over and the natural man is an enemy to God. Lust is an enemy to God's eternal plan because it draws the person involved away from the true God. When that happens, lust becomes the person's false god.

Whatever the compulsive sexual behavior a person chooses, the end results are inevitably feelings of worthlessness, despair, discouragement, failure, low self-esteem, hopelessness, frustration, and loneliness. The person in this position tends to feel that all is lost, that they can never be forgiven, so why should they try anymore?

Lust is Satan's counterfeit for love. Elder Richard G. Scott said, "Satan promotes counterfeit love, which is lust. It is driven by a hunger to appease personal appetite. One who practices this deception cares little for the pain and destruction caused another. While often camouflaged by flattering words, its motivation is self-gratification." (*Ensign*, May 1991, p. 35)

The world would have us believe that lust and love are the same thing.

The movies of today, the lyrics of many songs, the day-time shows, magazine articles, or novels often use the word love, but they depict Satan's counterfeit of lust. In a nutshell the world says that love equals sex. The Lord's definition is quite different. He says that love plus marriage equals wholesome sexual relations.

The Apostle Paul defined true love in his writings to the Corinthians. Love is the Greek word for charity. On the left side of the following chart are the Apostle Paul's definitions of love. On the right side, I've written what I believe to be Satan's counterfeit for love, which is lust.

Love   Lust
(1 Corinthians 13: 4–8)

Love	Lust
1. Charity suffereth long, and is kind.	1. Lust bails out and is mean.
2. Charity envieth not.	2. Lust always envies.
3. Charity vaunteth not itself, is not puffed up.	3. Lust is boastful and arrogant.
4. Doth not behave itself unseemingly.	4. Does indecent and inappropriate things.
5. Seeketh not her own, is not easily provoked.	5. Lust craves itself, is irritable and selfish.
6. Thinketh no evil.	6. Bathes itself in evil.
7. Rejoiceth not in iniquity, but rejoiceth in the truth.	7. Enjoys iniquity more than truth.
8. Beareth all things.	8. Can't handle most things.
9. Believeth all things.	9. Believes what it wants; lies.
10. Hopeth all things.	10. Loses all hope.
11. Endureth all things.	11. Gives up; why try?
12. Charity never faileth.	12. Lust fails.

Lust is very addictive. A person can develop lustful thoughts at a very early age. In the *Strength of Youth* pamphlet, the Lord has told us through his prophets to abstain from premarital sex, petting, necking, sex perversion, masturbation, and preoccupation with sex in thought, speech, and action. All these are manifestations of lust.

A FRIEND'S STORY

I've discussed the effects of lust in one's life and the pattern of a compulsive sexual lifestyle. Here is a real-life story about a man who had a compulsive sexual cycle that spanned over fifty-four years. I hope by sharing his experience, you can identify how he got into this compulsive sexual lifestyle and how he finally began to make changes, surrender his weaknesses, and build a Christ-centered life. His story shows that it is never too late. No matter how long a pattern has been going on, with the Lord's help, it can be changed. As you read through his story try to identify the compulsive sexual patterns in this man's life.

• • •

When I was eleven or twelve years of age, a boy moved into our town who had a vivid imagination. I had never masturbated in my life and didn't know what the word meant until many years later, but this boy introduced me to masturbation.

I had become "hooked" within hours of this new experience and only learned fifty-four years later that I had become a sex addict without any idea of the continual problems this would cause me. Lust had easily found a home in my heart and mind without giving me a single clue to what was happening to me. In a few short years, I knew that what I was doing was wrong, but the excitement and pleasure that I experienced from playing this new "game" eclipsed my feelings of guilt and remorse.

After each episode of masturbation, I experienced greater guilt and remorse and I resolved hundreds of times to give up masturbation, because I knew it was terribly wrong, but I could not do so. I decided to give reality a chance. I was married in the temple. I was positive that I had changed my behavior and was ready for marriage. Looking back on my life, it was not surprising to me how warped my thinking became. I had fantasied sexual relations so often and thought marriage would fulfill everything that I had imagined. Later in life and long after I was married, I finally realized that the realities of sex could not possibly equal the fantasies I had stored over many years in the memory bank of my brain.

I knew I had married the right woman but within a year lust prevailed.

I was again looking for the woman of my fantasies who could solve all my problems and "cure" me. I was a good dancer and before long I was looking for opportunities to meet women who fit my fantasy images. I could now claim "victory" over masturbation, but found I had replaced my desire for masturbation with the much more serious sin of seeking out and being with other women.

In my work I traveled a lot. I was a corporate

attorney that specialized in product liability. In my travels, I found many opportunities to meet other women. Each time I made a connection with another woman, I was sure she could cure me and solve all my problems, but I soon found this was not true.

After each acting out episode, guilt and remorse lasted for weeks, but with Satan's help I soon found another woman. In looking back, it does not surprise me that there were dozens of one-night stands in my life, each ending with longer periods of guilt. Before long, Satan would tell me there would be even greater possibilities the next time. I kept all of this secret.

During the years of my compulsive sexual behavior, I went through the church disciplinary system three times. I denied that I had a problem with my sexual behavior during the seventeen years of rearing our children. During this time, I did not act out on my thoughts, but they were still there. I thought since I wasn't acting out, I was cured.

After seeing my first child leave the nest, I found I had never been able to give up my fantasies completely and I started anew to seek a cure and someone who could solve my problems. At age sixty-six, I found a twelve-step support group for individuals who wanted to overcome their sexually compulsive lifestyles. Attending the support group was the first step in recognizing that I was an addict. I was addicted to sex.

Once I realized that it was my problem, I could then take the difficult but necessary steps that would allow me to change.

I credit my wonderful wife for never giving up on me and creating a desire in our children to always love the Lord and His gospel.

After a few years of sobriety and following the painful, yet joyous path of complete repentance, I was ready to serve a mission. My wife and I had a wonderful experience in the mission field. I served as Branch President during most of our mission.

I now know that the temptation to act out my fantasies may always be with me, but I gain control of the obsession as I stay focused on the Savior.

When I am actively serving the Lord and trying to keep His commandments, Satan and his legions have little influence on me. They may and do tempt me. Nevertheless, I am at the helm and control what I think and do.

Without Christ and His gospel, I am sure I would not have this control. It was only after I surrendered my addiction to the Lord and made an honest and sincere effort to keep all of His commandments that I found the Lord would and could help me overcome my addiction. I have also found that if I keep my promises to the Lord, Satan's influences cannot overcome me, but if I fail to keep my promises, Satan's influence comes right back into my life.

• • •

As I indicated earlier, no matter how long a pattern has been going on, with the Lord's help it can be changed. It may sound as though it was too easy for this man to change. From the time he recognized and accepted that his problem was a compulsive sexual addiction and began the repentance process and began striving to live a Christ-centered life, it was nearly five years until he was victorious. I say this to indicate that repentance is a process, and it is rarely easy. There are no quick fixes. The time period should not discourage an individual seeking recovery. Repentance is an individual process between you, the Lord and your ecclesiastical leaders and every case is different. Never give up hope; no matter how long or short the process, repentance *is* possible.

THE COMPULSIVE BEHAVIOR PATTERN

Now let's summarize this man's compulsive sexual pattern.

First, he learned the behavior.

- A boy who had moved into town introduced him to masturbation.

Second, he used it to cover up unresolved feelings and out-of-balance emotions.

- He used lust to cover up the pain of guilt and remorse.
- Over several years of masturbation, he had developed fantasies and expectations about sexual relations within marriage that could not be met.
- Masturbation no longer deadened the feelings of guilt and remorse.
- He used women in hopes they would make him feel better about himself.

Third, he denied that his behavior was a problem; he was not ready to accept responsibility for his problem.

- He lived in denial for many years. He did not admit that he had a problem.
- He didn't realize until years later that he was hooked on lust.

Fourth, he never told anyone about it (isolation).

- He never told anyone that he masturbated, though he knew it was wrong.
- Although he had been involved with other women, he initially didn't tell anyone.

Fifth, he used the compulsive behavior again and again.

- He resolved hundreds of times to give up masturbation, but couldn't.
- Although he was married, he sought sexual relationships with other women.

This is the cycle of a compulsive behavior. To get out of this compulsive behavior, a person needs to begin the following process.

SURRENDER THE WEAKNESS TO CHRIST AND BEGIN A CHRIST-CENTERED LIFE

First, he realized that he needed help and sincerely sought it out.

- He realized that he had a problem and that he needed to do something about it.
- He sought help for his problem.

Second, he surrendered to Christ and began a Christ-centered life.

- He started living the gospel as best he could and followed the complete repentance process.
- He controlled his sexual obsession by staying focused on the Savior.
- He surrendered his addiction to the Lord and made an honest and sincere effort to keep all the commandments.
- He replaced his acting out by serving the Lord and striving to keep His commandments.
- He has now kept his promises to the Lord as best he can.

USING THE DRUG TO COVER UP UNWANTED FEELINGS

People who have been in a compulsive sexual lifestyle attempted to use this behavior to cover-up feelings or emotions that they did not like or want to feel. It was their way of placing their feelings in a dark closet and pretending that they did not exist. As long as they were acting out and going to the grain bin, they didn't feel unwanted feelings, but the feelings kept coming back whenever they were away from the grain bin. They never told anyone about their compulsive behavior. They kept it a secret for a long time. Finally, the guilt and pain were just too much and they sought help.

TRIGGER POINTS

I refer to out-of-balance emotions as trigger points that cause you to reach for the drug of lust.

What are some feelings or emotions that you have tried to cover up with your compulsive sexual behavior?

1. Loneliness
2. Anger
3. _____
4. _____
5. _____
6. _____
7. _____
8. _____
9. _____

SUPPORT GROUPS

Because of the number of years they had been in the compulsive cycle and the seriousness of their transgressions, some people I have worked with needed more support and help than I could give them. Consequently, they chose to attend support groups; some found them helpful.

However, before you make the decision to attend a support group, I caution you to prayerfully determine what's best for you and discuss the matter with your bishop. Not everyone who has attended a support group has had an uplifting and beneficial experience. Being open with your bishop, the Lord, and trusted friends who can provide you with a safe place to share your feelings is the beginning of a desirable support system.

Eventually, we want to surrender to the Lord all of our out-of-balance emotions. He is our best friend and support.

THE TEN STEPS

Recovery and a Christ-centered life won't be easy and at times the progress may seem very slow—almost unnoticeable. Keep going. Keep trying. Today is the beginning. The sun will shine again. The perfect brightness of hope will appear. You and the Lord will make a great team. You can begin today to choose a Christ-centered life.

How can you surrender your inappropriate behavior to Christ and begin to feel His unconditional love? The following ten steps can assist you. If you choose to take these steps, you will experience great progress toward living a Christ-centered life. Many people have found the power to surrender inappropriate sexual behavior through this process. The most important thing is to get started.

The following are steps to assist you in surrendering your compulsive sexual behavior and turning yourself to Christ in order to begin a Christ-centered life. Each step will be explained in a chapter of the book.

Step One

Be aware, admit that you have a problem, and accept total responsibility for it.

O my son, I desire that ye should deny the justice of God no more. Do not endeavor to excuse yourself in the least point because of your sins. (Alma 42:30)

Step Two

Realize that only through Jesus Christ can you be healed and enjoy peace and continued progress.

> *Will ye not now return unto me, and repent of your sins, and be converted, that I may heal you?* (3 Nephi 9:13)

Step Three

Strip yourself of pride and follow the complete steps of repentance.

> *And I also thank my God, yea, my great God, that he hath granted unto us that we might repent of these things, and also that he hath forgiven us of those our many sins and murders which we have committed, and taken away the guilt from our hearts, through the merits of his Son.* (Alma 24:10)

Step Four

Identify the irrational thinking that allowed you to continue this compulsive behavior. Work patiently to replace irrational thoughts with rational thoughts that are Christ-centered.

> *Condemn me not because of mine imperfection, neither my father, because of his imperfection, neither them who have written before him; but rather give thanks unto God that he hath made manifest unto you our imperfections, that ye may learn to be more wise than we have been.* (Mormon 9:31)

Step Five

Identify your trigger points and the places your compulsive sexual behavior takes place.

Behold, verily, verily, I say unto you, ye must watch and pray always lest ye enter into temptation; for Satan desireth to have you, that he may sift you as wheat. (3 Nephi 18:18)

Step Six

Surrender all of the negative emotions that have become your trigger points to Heavenly Father through prayer; avoid places or situations that become trigger points.

Preach unto them repentance, and faith on the Lord Jesus Christ; teach them to humble themselves and to be meek and lowly in heart; teach them to withstand every temptation of the devil, with their faith on the Lord Jesus Christ. (Alma 37:33)

Step Seven

Begin to use your relationship with Heavenly Father and Jesus Christ to fill your emotional needs and to replace trigger points. Plan your week in advance with Christ-centered choices that are positive replacements for your trigger points.

And now, my sons, remember, remember that it is upon the rock of our Redeemer, who is Christ, the Son of God, that ye must build your foundation; that when the devil shall send forth his mighty winds, yea, his shafts in the whirlwind, yea, when all his hail and his mighty storm shall beat upon you, it shall have no power over you to drag you down to the gulf of misery and endless wo, because of the rock upon which ye are built, which is a sure foundation, a foundation whereon if men build they cannot fall. (Helaman 5:12)

Step Eight

Know that God and Christ love us unconditionally even with our weaknesses. As we turn to Christ, He will make our weaknesses become strengths.

And if men come unto me I will show unto them their weakness. I give unto men weakness that they may be humble; and my grace is sufficient for all men that humble themselves before me; for if they humble themselves before me, and have faith in me, then will I make weak things become strong unto them. (Ether 12:27)

Step Nine

Fast at least monthly and establish and commit to a regular physical exercise program.

Organize yourselves; prepare every needful thing; and establish a house, even a house of prayer, a house of fasting, a house of faith, a house of learning, a house of glory, a house of order, a house of God; That your incomings may be in the name of the Lord; that your outgoings may be in the name of the Lord; that all your salutations may be in the name of the Lord, with uplifted hands unto the Most High. (D&C 88:119–120)

Step Ten

Keep trying and never give up hope.

Wherefore, ye must press forward with a steadfastness in Christ, having a perfect brightness of hope, and a love of God and of all men. Wherefore, if ye shall press forward, feasting upon the word of Christ, and endure to the end, behold, thus saith the Father: Ye shall have eternal life. (2 Nephi 31:20)

Record your thoughts concerning applying the Ten-Step process to your own recovery.

_____

_____

_____

_____

_____

_____

_____

1

It's My Problem

Be aware, admit that you have a problem, and accept total responsibility for it.

O my son, I desire that ye should deny the justice of God no more. Do not endeavor to excuse yourself in the least point because of your sins. (Alma 42:30)

Recovery—a change of heart within a person—cannot begin until the person admits that he has a problem. If a person cannot honestly say, "This is who I am and this is what I've done," he cannot begin the steps that lead him out of the compulsive behavior. Once he takes ownership for his actions by admitting to himself that he has a problem, he is on the pathway to a Christ-centered life. Whatever the type of inappropriate sexual behavior a person chooses, this compulsive cycle continues repeatedly until the person surrenders his weakness to Christ and begins recovery through a Christ-centered life. Admitting and confessing to your bishop is the beginning of recovery.

The first step to confession is to admit that it's *your* problem. It's not your friend's problem. It's not your parents' problem. It's not your teacher's problem. It's not your spouse's problem. Recovery is impossible as long as you deny the seriousness of the problem or blame others for your actions.

Denial

Those who deny that they have a problem, stay in the compulsive sexual cycle. When you blame others, you excuse yourself, disown responsibility for your actions, and convince yourself that you don't have to do anything about them. This is one of Satan's great deceptions.

> *O my son, I desire that ye should deny the justice of God no more. Do not endeavor to excuse yourself in the least point because of your sins.* (Alma 42:30)

Denying that you have a problem, denying that you are responsible for it, or making the choice not to confess sins are ways to rationalize that serious problems are not that serious.

Rationalization

Here are typical things people say to themselves to rationalize their compulsive sexual problem and to convince themselves that they do not need to confess:

- If I didn't have so much stress, I wouldn't be doing this.

- My parents never talked to me about sex. Everything I learned, I learned from someone else. I can't help the way I was raised. If my parents had explained more about sex, I would have the proper attitude now.

- If my parents had taught me that masturbation was wrong, I wouldn't be doing this.

- If my parents had talked to me about sex, I would have grown up with a proper attitude about sex and I wouldn't be seeking a homosexual partner.

- It's the only thing that gives me real pleasure in life.

- I'm going to stop on my twenty-second birthday.

- I'm going to give myself a present this Christmas season and stop.

- I'm going to stop when I move into the new apartment.

- This will be the last time and then I'll never do it again.

- If my father had not been so emotionally distant, I would not have been involved in gay relationships.

- It's going to be my New Year's resolution to stop.

- If I do it enough times, I'll get so sick of it I won't want to do it anymore.

- My spouse never initiates sex. I'm always the one who has to initiate it. Why do I always have to be the one to initiate sex? I wouldn't do this if my wife was more responsive sexually or more interested in sex.

- My date initiated it. I would not have done it, but he started it.

- If I didn't have to travel, I wouldn't do this.

- If my mother had been more nurturing, I would not have thoughts of a lesbian relationship.

- I only do this with people I have real feelings for. It's not like I do it with just anyone.

- If I really want to, I can stop any time.

- It's just not the right time to try and stop. I'll stop after this semester.

This is only a partial list of ways we rationalize. You know yourself very well. You are the expert at identifying the ways *you* have rationalized.

You know them well because you have used them time and time again. List ways you have rationalized to deny that you have a serious problem. The more direct and open you can be, the better. It will be easier for you to begin a Christ-centered life by being as specific and honest as possible.

Don't beat yourself up over this, but determine to learn from what you have done in the past and use it to improve your future. List all the ways you can think of that you have denied that you have a problem or excused yourself from responsibility to solve it or rationalized in any way for not stopping NOW.

1. _____

   _____

2. _____

   _____

3. _____

   _____

4. _____

   _____

5. _____

   _____

Great inventions and significant changes have been made because inventors and others have learned from the past. You can learn from your past. You are an inventor. You can create a Christ-centered life. You have the power within you to create a new lifestyle and reach out and accept what Christ has offered you—His Atonement and His unconditional love.

The Healing Begins with *Christ*

————◆◆◆————

Realize that only through Jesus Christ can you be healed and enjoy peace and continued progress.

Will ye not now return unto me, and repent of your sins, and be converted, that I may heal you? (3 Nephi 9:13)

WE CAN'T HEAL OURSELVES

This scripture says that Christ will heal us. We won't and can't heal ourselves. If you try to heal yourself without the power of Jesus Christ, you will experience severe ups and downs and be driven about as chaff before the wind: "*For behold, the Spirit of the Lord hath already ceased to strive with their fathers; and they are without Christ and God in the world; and they are driven about as chaff before the wind.*" (Mormon 5: 16)

But behold, I was without hope, for I knew the judg-
ments of the Lord which should come upon them; for
they repented not of their iniquities, but did struggle for
their lives without calling upon that Being who created
them. (Mormon 5:2)

Once we realize it is only through God and Christ that
we can be healed, how can we call upon Them effectively?
One way is to pray in gratitude for every little thing we see
as we drive in the car. For example, I'm thankful for asphalt
to drive on instead of a dirt road. I'm grateful for this car
that gets me where I need to go. I'm grateful for school
buses that take kids to school. I'm thankful for school
teachers who teach my children.

We can also pray in behalf of harassed drivers, those we
see on the streets who look careworn, our own family
members who have pressing needs, etc. If it takes twenty
minutes to get to work, we have prayed for twenty minutes over every little thing that we see as well as our loved
ones who are on our minds. We begin to put God and
Christ first in our thoughts. Our thoughts turn to actions.
Our actions become more Christlike.

List ways you have learned to look to Christ and call
on Him for healing of your out-of-balance emotions, or
write down some things you would like to try.

1. _____

2. _____

3. _____

4. _____

5. _____

6. _____

7. _____

8. _____

9. _____

10. _____

As you turn to Heavenly Father and Jesus Christ, healing can begin. The Spirit will begin to influence you so you can control the natural man. *"For the natural man is an enemy to God, and has been from the fall of Adam, and will be, forever and ever, unless he yields to the enticings of the Holy Spirit, and putteth off the natural man and becometh a saint through the atonement of Christ the Lord, and becometh as a child, submissive, meek, humble, patient, full of love, willing to submit to all things which the Lord seeth fit to inflict upon him, even as a child doth submit to his father."* (Mosiah 3:19)

Mormon speaks of the Nephites and their relationship with Jesus Christ and says, *"They were once a delightsome people, and they had Christ for their shepherd; yea, they were led even by God the father."* (Mormon 5:17)

In the next verse, Mormon describes the deterioration of the Nephites' relationship with Christ. *"But now, behold, they are led about by Satan, even as chaff is driven before the wind, or as a vessel is tossed about upon the waves, without sail or anchor, or without anything wherewith to steer her; and even as she is, so are they.*" (Mormon 5:18)

Christ is the compass. He gives us direction. Through Him, the wind ceases, the rough waters are made smooth, and there is a great calmness. Seek that calmness. "*Ask, and it shall be given you; seek, and ye shall find; knock, and it shall be opened unto you.*" (Matthew 7:7)

Reflect on moments in your life when you felt great calmness and the spiritual steps you took to achieve it.

_____

_____

_____

_____

_____

_____

_____

Humility—The Foundation of Repentance

———◆———

Strip yourself of pride and follow the complete steps of repentance.

> *And I also thank my God, yea, my great God, that he hath granted unto us that we might repent of these things, and also that he hath forgiven us of those our many sins and murders which we have committed, and taken away the guilt from our hearts, through the merits of his Son.* (Alma 24:10)

DEVELOPING HUMILITY

Just as faith precedes the miracle, humility precedes repentance. President Spencer W. Kimball was a wonderful example of humility. He said:

> Humility develops through prayer and study. Somebody asked me this morning, "How do you

keep humble? Sometimes I am humble and sometimes I am unhumble." How do you keep humble? I think there is a formula that will never fail. First, you evaluate yourself. What am I? I am the circle. I am the hole in the doughnut. I would be nothing without the Lord. My breath, my brains, my hearing, my sight, my locomotion, my everything depends upon the Lord. That is the first step and then we pray, and pray often, and we will not get up from our knees until we have communicated. The line may be down; we may have let it fall to pieces, but I will not get up from my knees until I have established communication—if it is twenty minutes, if it is all night like Enos. If it takes all day long, you stay on your knees until your unhumbleness has dissipated, until you feel the humble spirit and realize, "I could die this minute if it were not for the Lord's good grace. I am dependent upon Him— totally dependent upon Him," and then you read the scriptures.

Could you read these scriptures . . . and not be lifted and inspired? . . . Well, you can create humility, and humility has to be fed, too, in the same way, with the right kind of vitamins. And when you have success, you do not glory in it for you, you glory in it for the Lord. (*The Teachings of Spencer W. Kimball*, p. 233)

REPENTANCE

Humility is the key that unlocks the door of repentance. We have the power to unlock the door. Repentance is a step-by-step process. It is not done in a few days or weeks. As we unlock the door, Christ will greet us with open arms and lift us up. Elder Theodore M. Burton said:

> The meaning of repentance is not that people be punished, but rather that they change their lives so that God can help them escape eternal punishment and enter into His rest with joy and rejoicing. If we have this understanding, our anxiety and fears will be relieved. Repentance will become a welcome and treasured word in our religious vocabulary.
>
> Our struggles to repent may cost us agony of mind and body also, but our commitment to our Heavenly Father to do His will will make repentance possible and bearable for us. In our repentance, we should remember that the Lord does not punish us for our sins; He simply withholds his blessings. We punish ourselves.
>
> How grateful we should be for a kind, wise, loving Savior who will help us overcome our faults, our mistakes, and our sins. He loves and understands us and is sympathetic to the fact that we face temptations . . . God is merciful; He has provided a way for us to apply the principle of repentance in our lives and thus escape the bondage of pain, sorrow, suffering, and despair that comes from disobedience. After all is said and done, we are God's sons and daughters. And for those who understand its true meaning, repentance is a beautiful word and a marvelous refuge. (*Ensign,* August 1988, p. 8–9)

Let's review the process of repentance:

Recognize and Admit Our Mistakes

We need to admit that we have made mistakes. We cannot begin the repentance process without humbling ourselves and admitting our mistakes.

Feel Sorrow for Our Sins

The scriptures and prophets teach that we need to have a "broken heart and a contrite spirit" to fully repent. The sorrowing should be because we have violated God's laws. President Benson explained the big difference between godly and worldly sorrow.

> I would like to stress . . . what the scriptures term "godly sorrow" for our sins. It is not uncommon to find men and women in the world who feel remorse for the things they do wrong. Sometimes this is because their actions cause them or loved ones great sorrow and misery.
>
> Sometimes their sorrow is caused because they are caught and punished for their actions. Such worldly feelings do not constitute "godly sorrow." Godly sorrow is vividly portrayed in two places in scripture. In the final days of the Nephite nation, Mormon said of his people: *"their sorrowing was not unto repentance, because of the goodness of God; but it was rather the sorrowing of the damned, because the Lord would not always suffer them to take happiness in sin. And they did not come unto Jesus with broken hearts and contrite spirits, but they did curse God, and wish to die."* (Mormon 2:13-14)

In the Eastern Hemisphere, the Apostle Paul labored among the people of Corinth. After reports came of serious problems among the Saints, including immorality (see 1 Cor. 5:1), Paul wrote a sharp letter of rebuke. The people responded in the proper spirit, and evidently the problems were corrected, for in the second epistle to them, Paul wrote: *"now I rejoice, not that ye were made sorry, but that ye sorrowed to repentance: for ye were made sorry after a godly manner . . . For godly sorrow worketh repentance to salvation not to be repented of: but the sorrow of the world worketh death."* (2 Cor. 7:9–10.)

In both of these scriptures, godly sorrow is defined as sorrow that leads us to repentance. Godly sorrow is a gift of the Spirit. It is a deep realization that our actions have offended our Father and our God. It is the sharp and keen awareness that our behavior caused the Savior, He who knew no sin, even the greatest of all, to endure agony and suffering. Our sins caused Him to bleed at every pore. This very real mental and spiritual anguish is what the scriptures refer to as having a *"broken heart and a contrite spirit."* (See 3 Ne. 9:20; Moro. 6:2; D&C 20:37, 59:8; Ps. 34:18, 57:17; Isa. 57:15.) Such a spirit is the absolute prerequisite for true repentance. (*Ensign*, October 1989, p. 4)

Forsake Our Sins

We need to be willing to leave the old habits and sins behind. We sacrifice and surrender our sins to know Jesus Christ.

Confess Our Sins

Being open, coming out of isolation, telling your
bishop everything, is step one in your recovery. It is the
place to start. Complete and honest confession will bring
great relief. Satan wants you to believe that no one could
really love and care for you after what you have done. By
telling the bishop everything, you immediately clear up
this falsehood. The Lord loves you perfectly and unconditionally and His disciples have been commissioned to
reflect this love.

The process of confession won't be easy. As you
approach the church building, a hundred times you may
feel like turning the car around and returning home.
Don't turn back. Keep the appointment. It is the beginning of your Christ-centered foundation, the beginning of
your Christ-centered life.

How can you end your compulsive behavior without a
beginning? Can you ever reach the finish line without
first going to the starting blocks? Can you have a sunset
without a sunrise? Confession is your beginning. No one
can take it from you. Enjoy the peace that your new
beginning will give you.

When we confess our sins to our Heavenly Father and
our bishop, our sins begin to lose power over us. If we confess the little things we do, we have power from God that
will keep us from committing the more serious sins. If we
overlook the little sins, they will eventually lead us to committing more serious sins. Stripping ourselves of pride and
confessing our sins begins the repentance process. President
Benson said, "Think of the repentance that could take
place with lives changed, marriages preserved, and homes

strengthened, if pride did not keep us from confessing our sins and forsaking them." (*Ensign*, May 1989, p. 6)

Speaking about confession, Elder Theodore M. Burton said:

> Naturally, the confession that precedes repentance for serious sins should be made to a bishop or stake president who has the authority to hear such confession.
>
> Confessions to others—particularly confessions repeated in open meetings, unless the sin has been a public sin requiring public forgiveness—only demean both the confessor and the hearer. (*Ensign*, August 1988, p. 9)

The first place to begin the confession process is with your bishop. If your transgression has injured another person, confession to that person may be appropriate. However, you should be very selective when you share personal information about your transgressions with others. Full repentance may require you to confess to only a few people.

We need to realize that it may not be appropriate to discuss everything at once with loved ones. Innocent people, such as parents or a spouse, may not be ready to hear what we have done. Thoughtful and prayerful consideration should be made before you take the step to confess and make restitution. Be considerate of innocent people; don't dump everything on your parents or spouse just to make yourself feel better. Timing is important. Sensitivity is essential. When trust has been violated, it may take a long time to heal. A premature or inappropriate confession to a loved one, even with the hope of beginning the restitution process, can make the healing process more difficult. The bishop, through the spirit and mantle of his calling, can assist you in determining who you need to confess to; the rest of your friends or family don't need to know.

Confession to the proper church authority keeps us humble. It brings the sin into the light and Christ is the source of light. When we keep something hidden and don't confess it, we stay in darkness where Satan rules.

One real benefit of confession is that we immediately begin to feel better. When we feel better emotionally, we are less likely to fall into another trap. As we confess, the guilt and the burden of the sin immediately begin to be lifted from our shoulders.

Make Restitution

It is not just a matter of confessing at the right time in a sensitive manner. If our sins have injured other people, we need to make restitution. We need to restore, as much as possible, that which was lost because of our sins. Through the Spirit, and through counseling with your bishop, you will know the right time to confess and the right people to confess to. Once this is determined, full restitution of trust, honor, respect, covenants, promises, and fidelity need to be top priority. You are responsible to make restitution.

If another person chooses not to accept your restitution, it is his choice and his problem. But this should not discourage you from fulfilling the Lord's requirement and commandment to make full restitution to those involved. In some cases, praying for the other person may be the most appropriate way, for now, to make restitution.

Forgive Others

If we want forgiveness from our Heavenly Father, we must forgive others who may have injured us in some way.

> *Wherefore, I say unto you, that ye ought to forgive one another; for he that forgiveth not his brother his trespasses standeth condemned before the Lord; for there remaineth in him the greater sin. I, the Lord, will forgive whom I will forgive, but of you it is required to forgive all men.* (D&C 64:9–10)

Keep the Commandments and Endure to the End

Keeping the commandments gives us spiritual power. When we keep the commandments, we have the Holy Ghost to lead and guide us. We cannot endure mortality with all of its temptations without the full armor of God. We put on the armor of God as we obey His commandments.

Elder Theodore M. Burton said,

> In the Book of Mormon King Benjamin explains one way we can show our gratitude to the Lord for His great mercy and His sacrifice for our sins; '*Behold, I tell you these things that ye may learn wisdom; that ye may learn that when ye are in the service of your fellow beings ye are only in the service of your God.*' (Mosiah 2:17) God's work and glory is to redeem His children. If we participate in redemptive service to others, we can, in some small measure, repay Him for His blessings. (*Ensign*, August 1988, p. 9)

As we repent, we protect ourselves from an everlasting destruction.

And their hearts were swollen with joy, unto the gushing out of many tears, because of the great goodness of God in delivering them out of the hands of their enemies; and they knew it was because of their repentance and their humility that they had been delivered from an everlasting destruction. (3 Nephi 4:33)

Repentance is a blessing. In the process one turns from the path of darkness back to the path of light. When one chooses a new life the winter season ends and the spring begins. However, just as planting the seeds precedes harvesting the crops, repentance precedes peace of heart and mind. The Lord revealed the steps to repentance, and we must take them one step at a time. As you take the first step, it will give you the peace and confidence that you need to take the next step. A child who is learning to walk takes one step at a time. We are all children—children of God who are learning to walk in His footsteps.

List several specific things you can do to begin the repentance process.

1. _____

2. _____

3. _____

4. _____

4

Developing Christ-centered Rational Thoughts

—•◦•—

Identify the irrational thinking that allowed you to continue this compulsive behavior. Work patiently to replace irrational thoughts with rational thoughts that are Christ-centered.

> *Condemn me not because of mine imperfection, neither my father, because of his imperfection, neither them who have written before him; but rather give thanks unto God that he hath made manifest unto you our imperfections, that ye may learn to be more wise than we have been.* (Mormon 9:31)

Elder Marvin J. Ashton defined irrational thought patterns that cause people to continue their compulsive sexual behavior. He said:

Self-mastery must always triumph over self-deceit for us to taste the fruits of good cheer. One form of self-deceit is rationalization. We prevent the Lord from being with us because we stray from His paths and explain our actions by consciously or unconsciously making excuses. We say to ourselves, I did it just to see what it was like.

Everyone else was doing it. I didn't want to be different. There was no other way to be accepted graciously. Or, he made me do it. The companion-ship of good cheer is possible through the keeping of the commandments of God, not through rational-ization. (*Ensign*, May 1986, p. 68)

It's so easy to get caught up in rationalization. Rationalization allows us to minimize the seriousness of our choices. President Gordon B. Hinckley said,

Many a man who has partaken of forbidden fruit and then discovered that he has destroyed his mar-riage, lost his self-respect, and broken his companion's heart, has come to realize that the booby-trapped jun-gle trail he has followed began with the reading or viewing of pornographic material. Some who would not think of taking a sip of liquor or of smoking a cig-arette, have rationalized indulgence in pornography." (*Teachings of Gordon B. Hinckley*, p. 46)

Rational thought patterns that are Christ-centered keep us emotionally in balance. Each irrational thought that we have needs to be replaced with rational Christ-centered thoughts.

On the following pages are examples of irrational thoughts with Christ-centered rational thought replacements.

IRRATIONAL THINKING VERSUS CHRIST-CENTERED RATIONAL THINKING

Irrational Thinking

Everyone else is having sex before marriage and they seem to be doing okay. I can always get married in the temple later.

Rational Thinking

There are many, many youth and adults who stay morally clean and do not have sex until marriage. I want to have the Spirit with me when I choose a marriage companion. Moral cleanliness allows me to have the Spirit with me.

Irrational Thinking

I've always wanted to know what sex was like.

Rational Thinking

God provided a time to know what sex is like. The appropriate time is after marriage.

Irrational Thinking

I'm not a spiritual person.

Rational Thinking

The natural man is an enemy to God. With God's power and spirit, I can control my natural desires and begin to think more spiritual thoughts.

Irrational Thinking

I've never been able to control my compulsive sexual thoughts and sexual behavior.

Rational Thinking

I know with God's help, I can begin to make progress. Why do I always try to do everything by myself? It's not too late to begin a Christ-centered life. I can replace my compulsive sexual thoughts with Christ-centered thoughts. Minute-by-minute, hour-by-hour, day-by-day, I can make progress and become more Christ-centered in my thoughts.

Irrational Thinking

Church is always so boring. I never get anything out of it.

Rational Thinking

If I look at church as an opportunity to partake of the Sacrament and draw closer to Jesus Christ, it becomes very enjoyable and rewarding. I've noticed church is a lot more enjoyable when I feel the Spirit and I'm not packing around a lot of guilt. In the past I told myself church was boring to justify not going. The real reason I didn't go was that I felt guilty when I was there.

Irrational Thinking

I'm a compulsive sexual person. This is who I am. I need to accept myself as I am.

Rational Thinking

I am a son or daughter of God. God did not create me to be a compulsive sexual person. I learned this behavior on my own. God wants me to become like Him. I can make progress each day as I turn to Him.

Irrational Thinking

I don't understand the scriptures. I don't get anything out of them when I read them.

Rational Thinking

There are many things in the scriptures that I don't understand. There are many things in the scriptures that I do understand. I can begin to feel the Spirit as I read the scriptures. As I study with the Spirit, my understanding of the scriptures will improve. It's not going to happen overnight. It will take time.

Irrational Thinking

How could something that feels this good be so wrong?

Rational Thinking

There is nothing wrong or dirty about wholesome sex within a marriage relationship. God has asked us to use this sacred power only within the bonds of marriage. The sin occurs when I have sexual relations before or outside of marriage or when I engage in masturbation, viewing pornography or other lustful behavior.

Irrational Thinking

Sex is natural. If God didn't want me to have sex, why did He create my body this way?

Rational Thinking

God created our bodies. Our bodies have a purpose. Our bodies are gifts from a kind, loving Heavenly Father. The power to procreate and bring children into this world is the main reason our bodies are created the way they are. Wholesome sex within marriage is an expression of love and affection and is ordained of God. The problem occurs when I have sexual relations with someone to whom I am not married, or anytime I engage in any lustful thoughts or actions.

Irrational Thinking

I know God doesn't hear my prayers. How could He? I've done everything wrong.

Rational Thinking

I've made some mistakes. However, God still loves me. When I engage in compulsive sexual acts, I choose not to feel His love. I will take time each day to pray often and begin to feel His love for me and listen to the whisperings of the Spirit. I need to make this a priority. When I feel like praying the least is when I need to pray the most.

Irrational Thinking

I'm never going to change. I've had inappropriate sexual thoughts and feelings for years. Why should I try to hide or suppress them any longer?

Rational Thinking

With God's help, many people have surrendered sexual obsessions. Repentance is more than just stopping the behavior. Repentance and change of behaviors are very difficult. However, I was not sent to earth with these compulsive sexual thoughts. I learned them on my own. I can surrender these unwanted thoughts to God. The reason I've failed in the past is because I've always tried to do it by myself. With God's help, I can make progress, although at times my progress may seem slow. Moment-by-moment, hour-by-hour, day-by-day, my progress can continue.

Irrational Thinking

When I stop doing this, I will talk to my bishop.

Rational Thinking

I need the Spirit more than ever. If I talk to the bishop now, I can begin the road to repentance and have the Spirit with me to overcome this sexual obsession. Satan loves darkness. When I don't confess, I'm surrounded by darkness. Confession brings my problem into the light and Christ is the light.

Irrational Thinking

What is the bishop going to think of me? I've been living a double life.

Rational Thinking

The bishop is a human being with his own weaknesses. When he was ordained and set apart as a bishop he was blessed with a mantle and power from on high. He is blessed with the power of discernment and an outpouring of love. I want to do what God wants me to do no matter what others may think. My pride is stopping me from seeing the bishop. I'm confident the bishop will treat me as a son or daughter of God.

Irrational Thinking

No one is perfect. Everybody has at least one major weakness. Compulsive sex is my weakness.

Rational Thinking

I do have weaknesses. With God's help, I want to make my weaknesses become strengths. Christ has the power to make my weaknesses become strengths.

Irrational Thinking

The last time I did this sexual act, I told myself I would never do it again. Since I'm not going to do it again, I don't have to repent.

Rational Thinking

Each sexual transgression requires full repentance. Obedience, after committing sexual sins, is one step of repentance, but it's not the complete process. Forsaking the sin is one step to repentance, but it's not complete repentance. I will not have the full Spirit unless I fully repent and follow all of the steps to repentance, not just the ones I feel comfortable about.

Irrational Thinking

Having sex isn't as bad as doing drugs.

Rational Thinking

Since when is it more important to worry about the degrees of sin instead of the sin itself? I need to concentrate on overcoming my sexual compulsive behavior instead of comparing sins. Any transgression that prevents me from being my best self should be a top priority for me to overcome. Sexual sins are very serious sins. The scriptures and the prophets have told us that certain sexual sins are next to murder in their seriousness.

Irrational Thinking

It's okay to have sex when I'm in love with my partner.

Rational Thinking

If I really love this person, I will respect him and reserve sex for marriage. I'm sure there could be seeds of love, but I need to determine how I can nourish these seeds into full bloom. Right now, by having sex with this person, I'm not able to determine if there is real love, or if what I'm feeling is merely lust. Because I have violated the law of chastity before, my mind feels cloudy. I need to repent and move closer to Christ, so I can have the Holy Ghost to help me identify whether or not I am feeling true love for this other person.

Irrational Thinking

This person fills every need I've ever had. Sex is one of my needs. Naturally I want that one filled too.

Rational Thinking

There is no human being that can fill every need. Only God and Christ are perfect and can fulfill all our needs. I should try to improve my relationships with God and Christ instead of relying so heavily on another human being to fill my needs.

Irrational Thinking

This is the first time I have felt totally loved and accepted by another person. I don't want to lose him, and if I don't give him what he wants, he may leave.

Rational Thinking

I think I have tried to convince myself that I have never felt totally loved and accepted before by repeating those words over and over again in my mind, but I wonder if I have just deceived myself? Now that I think about it, I have had other experiences when I felt loved and cared for, but I have been blocking them out to justify continuing my sexual acting out. One reason I feel close to this person is because I have been open with him, but this kind of closeness is not likely to last. If I repent and begin a Christ-centered life, I can feel close to Christ. Only then will I be intact enough to sustain a feeling of closeness to someone else.

Irrational Thinking

Why go talk to the bishop? He has his own problems. I don't want to be a burden in the ward.

Rational Thinking

This is just an excuse so I don't have to repent. I'm really embarrassed about what I've done. Why do I always look for an excuse when my pride and ego are the real problems?

Irrational Thinking

If my spouse would have sex when I initiated it, I wouldn't be doing this right now.

Rational Thinking

My spouse is a human being with feelings and emotions. There are times when she just doesn't feel like having sex. She has that right. After I initiate sex, and if she's not interested, I need to talk to her about my feelings. If I feel rejected, I need to take responsibility for it and express these feelings to my wife. This will help me diffuse resentment and feel accepted, even though we may not have sex. It's okay to feel rejection, but it's not okay to choose a compulsive sexual behavior to cover up feelings of rejection. Expressing my honest feelings to my wife is a positive way to deal with them; giving her the silent treatment is a negative way.

Irrational Thinking

I can overcome this compulsive sexual desire and acting out by myself. I've done everything else that I've ever put my mind to.

Rational Thinking

I haven't been successful trying to do it myself. I've had several major setbacks. It's happening more often now than ever before. When am I going to humble myself, swallow my pride and go talk to the bishop?

Irrational Thinking

Drugs are illegal, but pornography is not. Society says it's okay. If it's not illegal, I should be able to do it.

Rational Thinking

Many things may be legal according to the laws of the land. There are God's laws and man's laws. We are asked to follow God and live His commandments. God has commanded us through His prophets to avoid pornography. Satan is the author of pornography even though another name may appear as the publisher. Satan is behind every pornographic magazine, video, or internet website that is pornographic in nature. Pornography allows the adversary to bind people with chains that become difficult to break. Christ has the key to break the chains and He will free us as we turn to Him.

Irrational Thinking

No one knows about this, so I don't have to repent. A person only has to repent for sins that other people know about.

Rational Thinking

I'm worried more about what others think about me than what God knows. God knows I've violated the law of chastity. Do I want to please God or man? I need to have more faith in God and Christ.

Irrational Thinking

Masturbation helps me to relax so I can go to sleep at night. If I don't sleep well, I don't have the energy I need to keep up with my school and work.

Rational Thinking

There are several choices I can make to relax myself. I have chosen to masturbate. Why not begin to make choices that help me to relax and also allow me to draw closer to Jesus Christ? I can write in my journal. I can listen to uplifting music. I can surrender my feelings and out-of-control emotions to Heavenly Father. I can ask Him to replace these feelings with calmness and relaxation. I can do some physical exercises just before I retire for bed. Masturbation makes me feel guilty and unworthy. I really can't be my best self when I'm packing around all of this guilt and shame. It uses up energy I could spend doing worthwhile things. I need to keep trying to overcome masturbation. The progress seems slow at times, but I know with the help of God and Christ, I can overcome it.

Irrational Thinking

The Church is so big. There isn't any personal touch. I feel like I'm just a membership number.

Rational Thinking

There are several million members in the Church. Christ still knows each one. I should really focus on the Savior and continue to develop my personal relationship with Him. The Church is a vehicle to help me develop my relationship with the Savior, but it's certainly not a replacement for the Savior.

Irrational Thinking

If I do a really good job in my church calling, the Lord will forgive me for what I've done.

Rational Thinking

It's important to put forth my best effort in my church calling, but that is not a substitute for taking the steps of repentance. To really be my best self, I need to follow all the steps of repentance. Service in God's kingdom does not replace repentance.

Irrational Thinking

It is okay to go dancing with women other than my wife since it is good exercise, and I can restrict my interaction with the other women to dancing only.

Rational Thinking

For many men, (and especially sexually compulsive people) dancing is foreplay and leads up to the sexual act. I am flirting and tempting myself when I engage in this activity. I need to avoid all activities of this nature.

Irrational Thinking

I feel there are so many hoops the bishop and stake president are requiring me to jump through to get back into the Church. It seems they don't really understand me as a person with individual needs.

Rational Thinking

The scriptures and the prophets speak about the "broken heart and contrite spirit." Have I really had a change of heart? Have I really received His image in my countenance? If my heart is in the right place, wouldn't I be more willing to follow the steps of repentance? I know there have been things they have asked me to do that I didn't want to do right then, but six months later, I saw the wisdom in the request. The process of repentance is so difficult at times. I still have feelings of being unacceptable, unworthy, and unloved. I will continue to try. I will not give up hope. I love the Savior. I want to feel His love. I know He accepts me. He knows what I've done. He loves me unconditionally. The bishop and stake president are His servants.

Irrational Thinking

If my parents, spouse, friends, or boss treated me better, then I wouldn't feel so angry or sad. That is what caused this problem.

Rational Thinking

I am not a victim. I am accountable for my own happiness and my own behavior. If I don't like how others treat me, I can express my feelings, ask for changes, accept the fact that others may not choose to change, and decide what I want to do next.

Irrational Thinking

I thought my sexual fantasies with women were real and should be realized in my life.

Rational Thinking

I have learned that my fantasies are based on lust, not reality. There is no limit to my imagination in this area, but there are many limits in reality. I need to differentiate between reality and fantasy and also realize the difference between lust and love. Lust is concentration on the physical and our desire to make it whatever we want it to be. Love is exemplified by the Lord and is concerned with the well-being and growth of all involved. We must restrict our sexual activities within our marriage covenants and remember that we are all children of God. To completely accept this principle leads us to appropriate thoughts and actions.

Irrational Thinking

I do not have to put up with my wife's weaknesses and failings in this life. I will get a divorce and then make sure I find another woman to marry who does not have the unacceptable weaknesses and failings my wife has.

Rational Thinking

The Lord expects us to try to reconcile our differences with our spouses. If we will do this, He will make our weaknesses our strengths. We marry in the temple for time and all eternity. It will not be easy, but it will be worth it.

Irrational Thinking

Sex outside of marriage must not be harmful because so many people do it and seem to suffer no dire consequences.

Rational Thinking

If we do not keep our sexual activities within the marriage covenant, we open the gates and invite Satan to tempt us. This is so serious a transgression in the eyes of God, that those who transgress not only must provide restitution but ask and receive the forgiveness of the Church and God Himself. The consequences may not be immediately apparent, but they are serious, indeed.

Irrational Thinking

There is no harm in telling a little lie to a woman—such as pretending that I am single. When a woman wants extracurricular activity as much as I do, she wouldn't expect me to marry her.

Rational Thinking

Very few women are looking for casual sex with a married man. Most of them are looking for true love and when they find that a married man has lied to them they feel betrayed, demeaned, and violated. These "little" lies may seem harmless to men, but in the eyes of God they are despicable, even unthinkable. If not truly repented of, they will prevent a person from ever being with God and having His Spirit.

Irrational Thinking

If I can't have sex with my wife, I'm not going to make it another day. I feel like I'm going to die without it.

Rational Thinking

The body needs food and water in order to survive, but sex is not essential for survival. There are many unmarried people who regularly date and who live the law of chastity. There are also many wonderful people who have never had an opportunity for marriage who live the law of chastity. There are some married people who cannot have sex, because of one of the partner's physical disabilities. I will not die if I don't have sex. I will die if I don't have water and food because they are necessities. Sex is not. My spiritual body can control my physical body.

Irrational Thinking

I hate going to church. The whole ward is full of hypocrites.

Rational Thinking

Everyone has weaknesses. I need to be patient with other people's weaknesses just as Heavenly Father is patient with my weaknesses. From time to time, I catch myself so focused on other people's weaknesses that I don't have time to deal with or think about my own. This is a trick I play on myself, so I don't have to do anything about my own weaknesses.

Irrational Thinking

My spouse doesn't love me because when I initiate sex he or she is not interested.

Rational Thinking

I have a lot of work to do on my thinking. I have burned into my mind this false statement: *Love equals sex.* Maybe it happened because of the books, magazines, or movies I've exposed myself to over the years. Wholesome sexual relations within marriage is one of the many ways a couple can express their love to each other, but it's not the only way. Perhaps I need to recognize other ways my spouse shows love to me and allow my spouse the freedom to say no to sex if the timing or mood is just not right.

Irrational Thinking

No one loves me. I always have to call someone and initiate activities with other people. No one ever calls me.

Rational Thinking

Each person has his or her own schedule and things that need to be accomplished each day. Just because a person doesn't call me, doesn't mean I'm not important. At moments such as this, I need to take the risk and call someone I know is good company and go enjoy a wholesome activity.

Irrational Thinking

I don't want to hurt this person's feelings, so I'm going to go out with him although I know he's not the type of guy I should be with.

Rational Thinking

Each person is responsible for how he feels. If I tell him no and he becomes angry or upset, it's his responsibility to deal with it and not mine. I need to take care of myself even if it means telling others no. It's okay to tell other people no. Who will take care of me if I don't? God expects me to protect and take care of myself.

Irrational Thinking

I don't have anything going this weekend, so I'm just going to call an old friend and see what's happening. Besides, I want to tell her happy birthday.

Rational Thinking

I've had problems every time I've taken this person out. Why am I setting myself up for another setback? How can I begin to help someone else if I can't help myself? I need to gain more strength and power through my relationship with Christ. If I do this, I won't need to use others for a crutch and subject myself to more problems and heartache. I won't call her because I don't want anymore pain.

Irrational Thinking

If I don't give this person what he wants, he is not going to like me anymore.

Rational Thinking

I want this person to like me because of who I am—my talents, my personality, my goals and ambitions in life. I don't want him to like me just because of my body. A relationship based on physical attraction alone won't last. I need to build my spiritual power by continuing my relationship with the Savior. It may be time to discontinue my relationship with this person. I'm headed in the wrong direction. I want to continue my relationship with Christ.

Irrational Thinking

I've done this so often, what difference does it make now if I do it another time?

Rational Thinking

I've made several mistakes. Some of my mistakes are very serious. Today can be the day to begin my Christ-centered life. Today can be the day to leave behind the pain, sorrow, and anguish. It won't be easy. I must start now. I can surrender this feeling that I have to reach for my "drug of choice" by surrendering this out-of-balance emotion to my Heavenly Father through prayer.

Irrational Thinking

I've gone this far. I'd just as well go all the way. What difference does it make now? I'm never going to make it, anyway.

Rational Thinking

I made a major mistake. I have to accept full responsibility for it. Full responsibility doesn't mean I beat myself up and tell myself that I'm no good. I'm not a loser. God sent me to earth to succeed. He had full confidence in me that I would learn from my experiences and draw on His power. I've made lots of good choices in my life and I need to give myself credit for them. I've also made some bad choices. I need to learn from these choices and know that God still loves me and He will help me draw on His power as I turn to Him.

Irrational Thinking

I'm no good. I'm not worthy of Heavenly Father's help. I have already prayed for this problem to go away and it hasn't. Prayer doesn't work for me.

Rational Thinking

Heavenly Father loves me unconditionally. I am the one who has flawed the relationship. He is still there. He will listen to me, no matter what I have done. I can begin drawing on Heavenly Father's power by looking around and identifying the things I'm grateful for.

Irrational Thinking

My situation isn't all that bad. I don't do my compulsive behavior all that often.

Rational Thinking

Lust is a progressive drug. It takes more and more to produce the same adrenaline level of excitement. It's much easier to surrender the desire and obsession in the earlier stages than later. Anything that takes away from the Spirit is a serious matter. If Satan can make me think it's not that big a deal, he's got me right where he wants me. I need to identify my past irrational thinking that caused me to stay in the compulsive sexual cycle.

Irrational Thinking

Some people are born tall, some short, some with brown eyes, some with blue eyes—I was born gay.

Rational Thinking

We are all children of God born innocent, clean and pure. This doctrine is reinforced when we look at the age of eight for baptism. Any child who dies before eight will inherit the celestial kingdom because he is innocent. I was not born gay. My environment and upbringing may have caused some distorted thinking, but I was innocent, clean, and pure when I entered this world and I am responsible for what I have chosen to do with my life. As I continue to build a Christ-centered life, I can overcome my desire for gay relationships.

Write down several irrational thought patterns you have used in the past.

Below each irrational thought pattern write a rational thought pattern that is Christ-centered.

Irrational Thought Pattern

_____

_____

_____

_____

_____

_____

_____

_____

Rational Christ-centered Thought Pattern

_____

_____

_____

_____

_____

_____

_____

Irrational Thought Pattern

_____

_____

_____

_____

_____

_____

_____

_____

_____

_____

Rational Christ-centered Thought Pattern

_____

_____

_____

_____

_____

_____

_____

_____

_____

_____

Irrational Thought Pattern

_____

_____

_____

_____

_____

_____

_____

_____

Rational Christ-centered Thought Pattern

_____

_____

_____

_____

_____

_____

_____

Thoughts turn to actions. I want good actions, so I
need to develop good rational thoughts that are Christ-
centered. A seed turns into a beautiful flower. I want to
plant the seeds of rational thought patterns so that I, too,
can blossom. I no longer want to droop, wilt, and be
blown away by every wind of doctrine. As the sun rises in
the morning the spring flowers open and face the sun. If I

cut a tulip from my flower bed and place it in a jar of water, it will turn and face the sun. It will follow the direction of the sun from morning to night. The rays from the sun cause the flower to open. As I turn to the Son of God I, too, can blossom.

List ways you can begin to follow the Savior and turn your life over to Him today.

1. _____

_____

2. _____

_____

3. _____

_____

4. _____

_____

5. _____

_____

5

$\mathcal{T}$he $\mathcal{R}$oot of the $\mathcal{P}$roblem

———◆———

Identify your trigger points and the places your compulsive sexual behavior takes place.

Behold, verily, verily, I say unto you, ye must watch and pray always lest ye enter into temptation; for Satan desireth to have you, that he may sift you as wheat. (3 Nephi 18:18)

TRIGGER POINTS

Trigger points cause out-of-balance emotions that tempt you to reach for the drug of lust. Elder Neal A. Maxwell has said, "Our whole selfish society tends to travel light, pushing away from anyone who might be an obligation—jettisoning 'used' friends, relatives, and even partners. This disposability is one of the final stages of selfishness in which the individual is not willing to risk a commitment of any enduring nature, nor to be depended upon for anything. Those whom sensuality has made into such ciphers must remember—in their efforts to erase their loneliness by being surrounded by sensations—that in the arithmetic of appetite, anything multiplied by zero still totals zero!" (*Morality*, Neal A. Maxwell, p. 25)

Those who do not identify their emotional trigger points, but instead continue to cover them up with the god of lust, can become an emotional zero. Here are some common trigger points that may help you to identify your own.

> **Trigger:** I've always been so independent. I don't want to ask for help from anyone.

> **Trigger:** I see girls outside wearing short shorts or tank tops.

> **Trigger:** I am so bored. There's nothing to do.

> **Trigger:** These things always happen to me. I get so sick and tired of being the person who always gets dumped on.

> **Trigger:** There is nothing exciting going on. Is this all there is to life?

> **Trigger:** Each time I stop to get gas, I can see the pornographic magazines behind the counter.

> **Trigger:** I feel hurt because they wouldn't listen to my feelings.

> **Trigger:** My friends want to go see an R-rated movie.

Trigger: I see a lingerie ad in the newspaper.

Trigger: I like to flirt with cute guys.

Trigger: If I don't have a boyfriend, I feel insecure.

Trigger: I've really worked hard lately and I deserve a reward.

Trigger: The weather is cold, wet, and rainy.

Trigger: I've just completed a project and feel good about what I have accomplished.

Identifying Trigger Points

Identify your personal trigger points and write them down. Think about each trigger point and see how it causes you to reach for your drug of choice—the drug of lust. For example: *I usually fall back into my old habits and patterns when I see a young lady wearing tight clothing.*

1. _____
    _____

2. _____
    _____

3. _____
    _____

Also, write down the places where your sexually compulsive behavior usually takes place. Locations can be trigger points. For example: *It usually happens when I am in bed just before I go to sleep*, or: *It usually happens when I am in a car with a particular young man.*

1. _____
   _____

2. _____
   _____

3. _____
   _____

4. _____
   _____

If you are having a difficult time identifying your trigger points, ponder the following questions. They may help you uncover some of your trigger points.

Who are you trying to run from?

What feelings or emotions are you trying to hide or cover up?

Who are you angry at?

When do you feel rejected?

When do you feel insecure?

Is there a direct correlation between your compulsive behavior and stress?

Has there been a major change in your life in the last several weeks or months?

What do you get from acting out this compulsive behavior?

How can you replace this compulsive behavior with a Christ-centered behavior?

Watch and be aware of your emotional trigger points. The trigger points mentioned in the parable were rejection, self-pity, anger, and guilt. The lamb could not stop going to the grain bin. This became a compulsive behavior. If the lamb continues this compulsive behavior, the very behavior handicaps him—it's as though he has a broken leg. He cannot move very fast with a broken leg and it will be easier for a wolf or coyote to attack him. By not identifying your emotions and trigger points, you become an emotional and spiritual cripple and an easy target for the attacks of Satan and his army.

When you identify your trigger points and choose to surrender them to Christ, you become like a lamb with four strong legs. By choosing the Christ-centered life, any person can become whole and become his best self—the person that God intended him to become. However, even though God greatly desires for you to become your best self, He will not take away your free agency.

President Kimball said, "We live in a sterile age, or so it seems—an age when young people [also older people] turn to sex to escape loneliness, frustration, insecurity, and lack of interest." (*The Teachings of Spencer W. Kimball*, p. 271)

Circle some of your trigger points from the following list and write in any additional trigger points you can think of.

1. Loneliness	7. Hunger	13. Boredom
2. Low self-esteem	8. Certain friends	14. _____
3. Resentment	9. Movies	15. _____
4. Stress	10. Bad thoughts	16. _____
5. Success	11. Self-pity	17. _____
6. Anger	12. Fatigue	18. _____

Unwanted Feelings are Okay

It's very important to know it's okay to have feelings of loneliness, anger, or sadness, but it's not okay to use a compulsive sexual behavior to try to drug these feelings. Nothing is wrong with the feeling or trigger point; the problem arises when we deal with the feeling or trigger point in a negative way. The following steps will teach you how to deal with out-of-balance emotions in a positive way that will help you draw on Christ's power and become your best self.

Planning the Week Emotionally

We plan our appointments every week. We write down all of the things that need to be done, but what about planning our week emotionally? That's right—think about the emotional out-of-balance things that could occur this week and plan in advance how you might deal with them in a Christ-centered way. Let's say, for example, that loneliness is a trigger point. It's a three-day weekend and you know all of your roommates are going home and you'll be the only one at the apartment. How can you deal with loneliness in a positive way? What Christ-centered activity can you plan in advance to deal with loneliness? Can you plan to go somewhere? Can you volunteer your time at a nursing home? Can you do some gardening for an elderly person? If you don't plan your week by anticipating your emotional trigger points, it won't take too long for them to snowball and get out of control. Out-of-balance trigger points and the inability to surrender them to God and Christ are the roots of a compulsive sexual lifestyle.

Remembering the Trigger Points

It's important to try to establish a way to remember your trigger points.

When I was in the third grade, my school teacher, Mrs. Swenson, was reading to us the book *Charlotte's Web*. I really loved Mrs. Swenson. In my eight-year-old mind I thought that one day Mrs. Swenson would divorce her husband and marry me. It never happened. Anyway, she was special to me and made me feel important. One day, after lunch, Mrs. Swenson came into the classroom and said, "I'm not going to be able to read to you today," and then she started to cry. I had never seen her cry before and I felt very sad. She continued, "President Kennedy was just shot. Please read quietly on your own." She had a box of tissues on her desk. I had seen her wipe her mouth or nose before, but I had never seen her wipe tears from her eyes. I wanted so much to comfort her, but I didn't know how. I felt helpless.

Although I was just a boy, this experience is still very vivid in my mind. It is a good illustration of the fact that emotional trigger points and out-of-balance emotions are learned when we are very young. I took the title of the book *Charlotte's Web* and changed the spelling to remind me of my trigger points. When I think of this experience, it does three things for me. First, it reminds me that my emotional trigger points were developed at a very young age. I know now what they are and I have the responsibility to do something about them. Second, it reminds me of a third grade teacher who loved me. I can still feel her soft touch on my shoulder as she looked at my school work and whispered, "Very good, Rodey, you are doing so much better." I needed to hear that. I love her.

Third, I can plan Christ-centered choices in advance around anticipated trigger points that might occur during the week.

S tress
H unger
A nger
R ejection
L oneliness
E mptiness
T ired
S uccess

W orry
E go
B oredom

By using the new spelling: "Sharlet," I can quickly remind myself of my trigger points. Think about a catchy phrase or group of words that will help you in remembering your trigger points. Please write down your phrase or key words. As you learn more about your trigger points, you may need to add more words to your phrase.

_____

_____

_____

_____

_____

_____

_____

If we fail to deal with our trigger points, we open the door and allow the devil an opportunity to sneak in. The prophet Joseph Smith said, "All beings who have bodies have power over those who have not. The devil has no power over us only as we permit him. The moment we revolt at anything which comes from God, the devil takes power." (*Teachings of the Prophet Joseph Smith*, Section Four, p. 181)

A FRIEND'S STORY

We've covered five of the ten steps. Now let's take a moment to reflect on what we have learned by reading a personal history of one man's compulsive sexual cycle. As you read this story, try to identify his trigger points as well as how he surrendered his trigger points to God and Christ and began a Christ-centered life.

• • •

Having righteous parents, I grew up attending a Protestant church every Sunday. My four grandparents and many generations before them attended church on a regular basis. This gave me a legacy of religious activity.

My religious activity and desire to do what was right seemed more intense than those of my friends. However, my friends were good people without any real desire to do evil.

These friends were from various parts of North America, including Canada, since my father was assigned every couple of years to a new location. After active duty as an officer in World War II, he chose to remain in the military.

As I grew up through my school years, including college, my major challenge was to deny myself of all inappropriate relationships with girls. I knew that some day I would marry and have a family, but for now the most important things were my own family, school, and athletics.

Throughout these years, I knew pornography was bad and usually refused to engage in it, although on rare occasions I found it impossible to abstain. At times, my mind would fantasize and I would develop strange desires. I suppose this was the start of my masturbation.

During my five years at the university and two

years in the military, my brief encounter with pornography, fantasizing, and masturbating had left me with strong desires that I believed would be satisfied with marriage. Marriage was always my goal and most of my thoughts about marriage were righteous.

While in the military, two important events happened. First, I was baptized into the LDS church and then I met and briefly dated my future wife while I was stationed in California. My next assignment was in South Carolina. We corresponded for several months and were later married in California.

My time in the military was over and I started working for an insurance company in Iowa. Prior to marriage, my masturbation would come and go depending on my condition. Once married, it seemed that none of my fantasies came true and masturbation was a needed relief from my frustration. Again, it would come and go over extended periods.

My activity in the LDS church was very extensive and my desire for a righteous life was very strong. Therefore, when these periods of frustration and masturbation came, I tried very hard to suppress them. I prayed often, read books, studied the scriptures, magnified my callings, and did extra work—still the habit would return. One thing progressed to another thing until I committed adultery and was excommunicated. Twice, I confessed these serious transgressions to Church leaders and tried to properly repent. After excommunication, I put forth constant effort to be active in the Church as a nonmember. This was a long process including much prayer, many meetings with priesthood leaders, scripture study, study from other books, meeting with counselors, etc. At times, the repentance process didn't move fast enough for me.

At times, my church leaders asked me to do certain things, like meeting with a professional counselor, that I wasn't sure were necessary. I worked very hard for a long period of time and was finally rebaptized as a member of the LDS church.

Jesus the Christ has knocked on my door often. He has extended His hand and encircled His arms of love around me. Often I have gone to Him for forgiveness. Now I must realize that He alone can carry me through each day—alone I cannot make it.

Without constantly reaching out for His help, knowing that my weaknesses are still with me, I would again fail. I must bear my cross and ask for the help of Jesus each morning in prayer. At night I must kneel by my bed to thank Him for His help and to ask His forgiveness for my shortcomings.

I must pledge each Sunday when taking the Lord's Sacrament to renew my covenants and return next Sunday ready to again take His Sacrament worthily. Thus, each day, I must think of His Atonement and remind myself that next Sunday I want to be ready and worthy to partake of His Sacrament with a clean mind, heart, and soul.

I must study the scriptures daily and liken them unto myself. As I ponder the many truths therein and apply them to myself, I renew my desire to do no evil. I must strive to find ways to serve Him and His other children. Charity to all and a desire to be more

Christlike is a daily requirement. If I am to become like Him, I must strive each day to do His will.

There is nothing that makes me happier than doing these things and attending all my meetings. Keeping His other commandments such as tithing, fasting, Word of Wisdom, etc. provide me the opportunity to serve Him, protect myself, and receive His blessings.

I am the beggar who is always in Jesus' debt. But I know that He loves me, and that through His redeeming grace and Atonement, I will be with Him and my family in the Celestial world. This must be my daily thought and goal.

I believe Christ and in His plan of salvation. He alone can help me overcome my bad habits and live a more Christlike life. He alone can give me peace, joy, and happiness.

• • •

The Compulsive Behavior Pattern

Let's apply the compulsive behavior cycle to this man's life.

First, he learned the behavior.
- I knew pornography was bad and usually refused to engage in it, although on rare occasions I found it impossible to abstain.
- My mind, therefore, at times would fantasize and I would develop strange desires. I suppose this was the start of my masturbation.

Second, he used it to cover up unresolved feelings and out-of-balance emotions.

- However, once married, it seemed that none of my fantasies came true and masturbation was a needed relief from my frustration. Again, it would come and go over extended periods.
- Prior to marriage, my masturbation would come and go depending on my condition.

Third, he denied that his behavior was a problem; he was not ready to accept responsibility for his problem.

- One thing progressed to another until I committed adultery and was excommunicated.

Fourth, he never told anyone about it (isolation).

- Masturbation would come and go over extended periods, but he never confessed and repented.

Fifth, he used the compulsive behavior again and again.

- Before marriage and during marriage, my masturbation would come and go depending on my condition.
- Once married, it seemed that none of my fantasies came true and masturbation was a needed relief from my frustration. Again, it would come and go over extended periods.

Surrender the Weakness to Christ and Begin a Christ-centered Life

Now let's look at the process that allowed this man to begin a Christ-centered life.

First, he realized that he needed help and sincerely sought it out.

- I confessed these serious transgressions to Church leaders and tried to properly repent.
- Without constantly reaching out for His help, knowing that my weaknesses are still with me, I would again fail.

Second, he surrendered to Christ and began a Christ-centered life.

- I must bear my cross and ask for the help of Jesus each morning in prayer. At night I must kneel by my bed to thank Him for His help and to ask Him for forgiveness for my shortcomings.
- I must pledge each Sunday when taking the Lord's Sacrament to renew my covenants and return next Sunday ready to again take His Sacrament worthily. Thus, each day, I must think of His Atonement and remind myself that next Sunday I want to be ready and worthy to partake of His Sacrament with a clean mind, heart, and soul.
- I must study the scriptures daily and liken them unto myself. As I ponder the many truths therein and apply them to myself, I renew my desire to do no evil.

- I must strive to find ways to serve Him and those who would become His children. Charity to all and a desire to be more Christlike is a daily requirement. If I am to become like Him, I must strive each day to do His will.
- I've been rebaptized as a member of the LDS church.

One purpose of including this personal history is to help you to identify where you are in the compulsive sexual cycle and more importantly how to get out. At any point during the cycle we can begin to make Christ-centered choices that allow us to surrender the behavior and begin a Christ-centered life. However, it's much easier to surrender the cycle in the early stages.

The longer we stay in the cycle, since the drug of lust is a progressive drug, the more lust it takes to produce the same level of excitement and adrenaline rush.

A FRIEND'S STORY

Here is another friend's story. Try to see how this lady used the drug of lust to cover up feelings that she didn't want to feel. Try to identify her trigger points, how she eventually took responsibility for them, and how she surrendered them to God and Christ.

• • •

I was born into a fine LDS family. I have always been puzzled about why I developed a sexual problem. I thought if I analyzed my problem, my behavior would change. It didn't. I do believe it was helpful to understand how my background influenced my choices. Perhaps my mother's addiction to prescription drugs (which started when I was a teenager) along with my family's denial of my mother's addiction, contributed to my confusion and anger. Perhaps the fact that my father was a distant man, though kind, contributed to my loneliness. But in the long run, I have learned that blaming my dysfunctional family, past or present, will absolutely stop my recovery. I must not perceive myself as a victim.

I used to see my problems outside myself, so the solution was also outside myself. Now I must take accountability for my life, my problems, my feelings, and my happiness. So this is how my story goes.

I was boy crazy from about the age of eleven, which seemed normal. I began dating at fourteen. After I had been going with one boy for some time, he touched me inappropriately. I was sick with guilt. Through sobbing tears, I prayed for forgiveness.

I dated a lot and found it was pretty easy for me to attract boys. I was popular and was nominated for queen of every dance. Yet inside I felt different and kind of lonely. I also hated what was going on in my family.

But when a boy wanted me and when I was in his arms, I felt great. I developed an unhealthy dependence on boys. A couple of years after the first incident of touching, it happened again with someone else. I was devastated. I loved the Lord and had a strong testimony; I was so ashamed.

I had been taught that to repent meant that I

would not commit the sin again and I had.

I became suicidal at sixteen. I felt I was going to hell anyway, so I might as well speed it up. Several times over the next twenty years I thought I was right and should have ended my life early. How sad I feel now to look back at such a confused child. Though depression made me feel so hopeless at the time, I have learned since that things inevitably change. No problem is too big to be overcome, and there is immense help for those who are willing to learn how to live a happy life.

I went out with the same boy most of the time after I was sixteen, and at nineteen, we had sexual intercourse. I don't even like to think about how emotionally disturbed I became. I was going to college and went to a psychologist and group therapy. But as I look back, it never mattered how distraught or seriously depressed I felt afterwards, the problem marched forward. I've learned that my depression and low self-esteem actually fed the problem and made it worse. The more guilt I felt, and the sadder I became, the more I wanted to be held and kissed and desired.

I began having sex more frequently with the same boyfriend from ages twenty to twenty-two. I tried desperately to break up with him, but I couldn't stick with it. Eventually, I became pregnant. One saying I've heard is that there are no accidents. I believe now that I chose to "have to" get married to a man who would treat me as badly as I felt I deserved to be treated. I had disappointed my parents, myself, and Heavenly Father. The combination of that shame and allowing myself to be treated badly by my husband set me up for a series of affairs that I could have never imagined. After a year of marriage, I was longing for old boyfriends. And by two years, I was having a full-fledged affair. I was sick with myself when I finally got out of it. I confessed to my bishop two or three years later. Though very supportive and encouraging, of course, he said that only Heavenly Father could forgive me and that I would feel in my heart when He had. I never felt that. I know now that Heavenly Father knew there was so much heartache still to come.

A few years later, I was seeing someone else. I threatened to kill myself if we went all the way, so he didn't. I guess I had so little faith in my own will power that I relied on his. But in a few years there was another man, then another and another. I had begun a spiral downward that I couldn't seem to stop with any amount of my own will power, or praying, or studying, or church service. The very fact that I tried so hard to stay close to the Church added to my shame.

I couldn't face Heavenly Father. For ten years, all I could do when I prayed was sob that I was sorry. I was never looking for another lover; apparently I just became overwhelmingly attracted to men. I tried to resist these feelings. I wouldn't act on a particular infatuation for more than a year sometimes, but eventually, I would succumb to the temptation. I thought it was some special trait or look that they possessed that made me so attracted to them—some chemical reaction between us. It was as if they had some magic which compelled me. Now I see that the problem was in me. I was emotionally unhealthy.

I became so accustomed to failing that I finally gave up fighting. I just flirted with anyone I wanted to and instigated relationships again and again. I had several encounters with the opposite sex and never confessed and fully repented.

The emotional and physical involvement varied. I almost never actually had sexual intercourse, but everything that leads up to it I really became hooked on. I usually ended the involvement, because I knew it was wrong, but I didn't seem to have the strength until after I knew I had their attention or affection. But this false type of intimacy is really just fantasy and never filled the emptiness inside me. It only caused more pain, thus perpetuating my problem.

I kept many such relationships alive for years by "staying in touch," because I was acting out of fear that my marriage would fall apart someday and I wanted a lot of options. Although I acted and dressed in a way that was meant to attract men, I rarely reciprocated with those who flirted with me. I wanted to win the hearts of those who were a challenge: as if I could somehow prove I was worth something if someone handsome, wealthy, or powerful wanted me—a poor substitute for the healthy self-esteem I lacked.

I disguised my sense of low self-worth by overachieving in many areas. My workaholic lifestyle helped to keep me running away from my problems. That and my romances kept me preoccupied. I could spend six months to several years in the cycle of a relationship. (I have noticed that this can happen to women whether or not they are married. But if they are not married, this seems normal in our society, and it may be harder to recognize as self-destructive behavior. Compulsive romances or emotional dependency drive people away from, not toward true intimacy, and the hole inside is never filled.) I used romantic intrigue as a diversion from addressing my problems. I used it as an alcoholic uses alcohol.

Eventually, I became driven to do the very thing that was causing me pain and making me hate myself. Those who do not understand addiction, I am sure, would ask me, "Why didn't you stop?" At some point my freedom of choice was gone. My early choices affected that, and my attitudes about life and religion affected that. I've learned that as the alcoholic has the choice to not take the first drink, I have the choice of changing my behavior before it leads to an affair.

For about twenty years I used the feeling of being hurt in my marriage to keep the subconscious excuse for needing the attention of other men. I kept fighting and crying and asking for my husband to change. But the reality is that I stayed and kept blaming him for my sadness. My own actions (or inactions) were to blame, but I didn't understand that at the time.

My depression and anger also affected my relationship with my children. Since I couldn't control myself (or my mother's addictions, though she had been dead for years from an overdose) I tried to control my children. Consequently, my oldest son and I fought bitterly every day. My life had become unmanageable in many areas. The deterioration of my family relations let me know I had to get help. I didn't know how to stop the merry-go-round. All I wanted to do was die.

It's been about ten years now since I changed my course and started a new spiral—this time upward. I had some therapy. I read some books about different aspects of my problems. I changed my attitudes about life. I learned that my attitudes and thought patterns *preceded* my feelings of anger, fear, depression, and self-hatred, which in turn led to acting out.

I chose to stop feeling like a victim and learned to ask for what I needed and set boundaries about unacceptable behavior towards me. I learned to recognize when I'm still blaming others. If I believe *they* have the problem, then I will believe that changing *them* is the answer. I finally recognized that the relevant question was: What was I willing to do to solve my own problems?

I learned that communication is extremely important to make my feelings and desires known; but to try to convince other people with thousands of words to change is a waste of time unless they choose to change. *And* I learned that waiting until other people are willing to change before I give myself permission to be happy makes me dependent on *their* behavior instead of my own.

Now I try to face life based on the AA Serenity

prayer: "God grant me the serenity to accept the things I cannot change, courage to change the things I can, and wisdom to know the difference." I now choose to face life's problems without running away. I choose to be honest about reality. I learned new tools for effective problem solving. But I couldn't have done any of this at all until I felt that I deserved to be happy and to be treated with love and respect.

I got into a group program that would help me stop my own misbehavior so that my self-esteem could start to grow little by little. I learned that my emptiness inside stemmed from self-hatred instead of from the way others treated me. It stemmed also from a spiritual void, because my actions stopped me from feeling Heavenly Father's love.

Above all, I learned that Heavenly Father loves me no matter what I have done. Although I flawed my relationship with Him, I can see now that He was always available at any point. I now have faith that I can ask for guidance and that I will get help.

I used to think that I was so bad that I was not worthy for my prayers to be answered, because I had pleaded for this problem to go away and it didn't go away. But now I believe that Heavenly Father was letting me learn the lessons that I had to learn and guided me to the answer when I was ready for it. I learned that I am utterly dependent on Him, and that my own will power is insufficient to solve my problems. And I am learning patience—to see a long-term picture of the process, and make sure I am pointed in the right direction, walking toward the light little by little, although I still make mistakes and suffer pain.

I find encouragement in the dark times from the fact that when I was suicidal so many years ago, Heavenly Father reached out to me and sustained my life. He surely knew that some fine children would come into the world through me and my husband. One son served a mission and became a Seminary teacher. One daughter served a mission. Though I felt so lost, Heavenly Father was always watching over me and my family.

I have learned that great things can come from the process of walking through the problem, accepting accountability, and being willing to work toward the solution. I have learned a happy, peaceful way of living in the midst of life's problems. I have now achieved what my romances could never provide—a true connection with myself, others, and Heavenly Father.

• • •

THE COMPULSIVE BEHAVIOR PATTERN

Let's compare this lady's personal history with the compulsive sexual cycle.

First, she learned the behavior.
- I was boy crazy from about the age of eleven.
- I began dating at fourteen.
- After going with a boy for some time, he touched me inappropriately.

Second, she used it to cover up unresolved feelings and out-of-balance emotions.

- I used romantic intrigue as a diversion from addressing my problems.
- I learned that my emptiness inside stemmed from self-hatred instead of how others treated me.
- I used to think that I was so bad that I was not worthy for my prayers to be answered, because I had pleaded for this problem to go away and it didn't go away.
- My workaholic lifestyle helped to keep me running away from my problems. That and my romances kept me preoccupied.

Third, she denied that her behavior was a problem; she was not ready to accept responsibility for her problem.

- My mother was addicted to prescription drugs. (So, it was my mom's fault.)
- My family's denial contributed to my confusion and anger. (So, it was my family's fault.)
- My father was a distant man, though kind and this contributed to my loneliness. (So, it was my father's fault.)
- I used to see my problems outside myself, so the solution was also outside myself.
- For about twenty years I used the feeling of being hurt in my marriage to keep the subconscious excuse for needing the attention of other men.

Fourth, she never told anyone about it (isolation).

- I had several encounters with the opposite sex and never confessed and fully repented.

Fifth, she used the compulsive behavior again and again.

- But in a few years there was another man, then another and another.
- I usually ended the involvement, because I knew it was wrong, but I didn't seem to have the strength until after I knew I had their attention or affection.

SURRENDER THE WEAKNESS TO CHRIST AND BEGIN A CHRIST-CENTERED LIFE

Now, let's look at the process that allowed this lady to begin a Christ-centered life.

First, she realized that she needed help and sincerely sought it out.

- I got into a group program that would help me stop my own misbehavior so that my self-esteem could start to grow little by little.
- Above all, I learned that Heavenly Father loves me no matter what I have done. Although I flawed my relationship with Him, I can see now that He was always available at any point. I now have faith that I can ask for guidance and that I will get help.

Second, she surrendered to Christ and began a Christ-centered life.

- Now I take accountability for my life, my problems, my feelings, and my happiness.
- I choose to face life's problems without running away.
- I choose to be honest about reality.
- I learned new tools for effective problem solving.
- I couldn't do any of this until I felt that I deserved to be happy and to be treated with love and respect.
- I learned that I am utterly dependent on Him, not my own will power.
- I am learning patience.
- I have to see a long-term picture of the process, and just make sure I am pointed in the right direction, walking toward the light little by little, although I make some mistakes and feel some pain.
- I learned that my attitudes and thought patterns preceded my feelings of anger, fear, depression, and self-hatred, which in turn led to acting out.
- I learned to stop feeling like a victim and ask for what I need and set boundaries about unacceptable behavior toward me.
- Although I felt so lost, He was always watching over me.
- I have learned that great things can come from the process of walking through the problem, accepting accountability and being willing to work toward the solution.
- I have learned what my romances could never provide—a true connection with myself, others, and Heavenly Father.

This is a special lady. She has been through so much and has learned how to find peace. It has not been a pleasant journey, but through the love and power of the Savior she has made progress.

You, too, will see progress. Continue your Christ-centered journey. He is there with open arms. He loves you with a perfect and unconditional love.

He can and will lift you when you feel you are not worthy of being lifted. He has given us so much.

The Savior said:

> For every one that asketh receiveth; and he that seeketh findeth; and to him that knocketh it shall be opened. (Matthew 7:8)

> Search the scriptures; for in them ye think ye have eternal life: and they are they which testify of me. (John 5:39)

> It is I; be not afraid. (John 6:20)

> Rise, take up thy bed, and walk. (John 5:8)

> If ye continue in my word, then are ye my disciples indeed; And ye shall know the truth, and the truth shall make you free. (John 8:31–32)

> I am the good shepherd, and know my sheep, and am known of mine. (John 10:14)

> He that is without sin among you, let him first cast a stone at her. (John 8:7)

> I, the Lord, forgive sins, and am merciful unto those who confess their sins with humble hearts. (D&C 61:2)

6

$\mathcal{S}$urrendering $\mathcal{N}$egative $\mathcal{E}$motions to $\mathcal{H}$eavenly $\mathcal{F}$ather

—◈—

Surrender all of the negative emotions that have become your trigger points to Heavenly Father through prayer; avoid places or situations that become trigger points.

Preach unto them repentance, and faith on the Lord Jesus Christ; teach them to humble themselves and to be meek and lowly in heart; teach them to withstand every temptation of the devil, with their faith on the Lord Jesus Christ. (Alma 37:33)

Usually people who suffer with a compulsive behavior have a severe case of pride, but don't realize it because they also have low self-esteem and do not see themselves as prideful or arrogant. *"But beware of pride, lest thou shouldst enter into temptation."* (D&C 23:1)

It's very difficult for a compulsive person to ask for help, not only from other honest and sincere friends, but more importantly from our Heavenly Father. Mormon had great concern over the Nephites because they were trying to do it all alone. *"But behold, I was without hope, for I knew the judgments of the Lord which should come upon them; for they repented not of their iniquities, but did struggle for their lives without calling upon that Being who created them."* (Mormon 5:2)

When we try to deal with our compulsive behavior without calling upon God, we struggle and struggle and struggle.

PROCESS OF SURRENDER

We need to surrender our out-of-balance emotions to Heavenly Father. We do not have the power to control them ourselves. When an unpleasant thought or out-of-balance emotion occurs, simply say, "Father in Heaven, I do not have the power to control this thought or emotion. I am surrendering it to Thee." For example, if you feel lonely say, "Father in Heaven, I feel lonely. I am surrendering this feeling of loneliness to Thee because I don't have the power to control it myself. I pray, Father, as I surrender it that my feelings of loneliness might be replaced with Thy love and Spirit." Surrendering is turning our unpleasant thoughts or out-of-balance emotions to our Heavenly Father through prayer. By surrendering our out-of-balance emotions to Heavenly Father, we lose the desire for sin. Elder Neal A. Maxwell said:

> Thus when people are described as "having lost their desire for sin," it is they, and they only, who deliberately decided to lose those wrong desires by being willing to "give away all [their] sins" in order to know God. (Alma 22:18) (*Ensign*, November 1996, p. 22)

In the Church we discuss consecration—giving all of our time, talents, and resources to further God's kingdom on earth. Can consecration also include surrendering to God all of our out-of-balance emotions? Elder Neal A. Maxwell said, "Consecration is the only surrender which is also a victory." (*Ensign*, November 1992, p. 66) But as you choose to surrender your out-of-balance emotions to Heavenly Father, you deal with them in a positive way and have victory. It's not part of the plan for Heavenly Father to take our emotions and thoughts from us. This would destroy our free agency. As you surrender your out-of-balance emotions to God, you are free of the thoughts and emotions and receive His power to make Christ-centered choices that will allow you to become your best self.

President Ezra Taft Benson used the example of King Lamoni's father to explain that we must forsake and surrender all sin to know the Savior and receive joy:

> I cite for you an example of a man whose life was changed to a more Christlike life after he earnestly desired such a change and sought the Lord's help.
>
> Lamoni's father was a king who had bitter enmity toward the Nephites. A great missionary by the name of Aaron—one of the sons of Mosiah—had come to the Lamanite nation to bring them the gospel. He proceeded to the king's home and subsequently engaged him in a gospel discussion about the purpose of life. Once the king became receptive to his message, Aaron taught him about Christ, the plan of salvation, and the possibility of eternal life. This message so impressed the king that he asked Aaron, "*What shall I do that I may have this eternal life of which thou hast spoken? Yea,*

what shall I do that I may be born of God, having this wicked spirit rooted out of my breast, and receive his Spirit, that I may be filled with joy." (Alma 22:15).

Aaron instructed him to call upon God in faith to help him repent of all his sins. The king, anxious for his own soul, did as Aaron instructed:

"O God, Aaron hath told me that there is a God; and if there is a God, and if thou art God, wilt thou make thyself known unto me, and I will give away all my sins to know thee." (Alma 22:18)

Now I want you, my brethren, to hear again this humble man's words: "I will give away all my sins to know thee."

Brethren, each of us must surrender our sins if we are to really know Christ. For we do not know Him until we become like Him. There are some, like this king, who must pray until they, too, have a wicked spirit rooted from them so they can find the same joy. (*Conference Report*, October 1983, pp. 62–63; or *Ensign*, November 1983, p. 43).

PRICES WE PAY

At times, weighing the prices we have paid for our compulsive behaviors allows us to see the need to surrender all our sins. Here are some of the prices people pay by engaging in this compulsive sexual behavior.

Following the list, please write-in the prices you have paid by hanging on to your own compulsive sexual behavior.

1. Well-balanced meaningful relationships with the opposite sex have been lost

2. Lost time from work and personal development.

3. Separation from spouse

4. Divorce

5. Money spent to feed the addiction

6. Peace and serenity lost

7. A relationship with the Savior lost

8. Feel alienation from the Church

9. _____

10. _____

11. _____

12. _____

13. _____

14. _____

15. _____

JARS OF GRAIN

If we continued our analogy of compulsive behavior in the Parable of the Lamb, we might find that one of the last times the lamb went to the grain bin, he took a jar of grain home with him and hid it where no one could find it. He thought that if he became really desperate, he could go to the jar and cover up his emotional pain.

Surrender means giving up the last two or three jars of grain we have hidden.

What are some examples of jars of grain that you might have hidden? It seems the last few jars of grain are the most difficult to surrender. At first you may have forgotten where you buried them. As you continue a Christ-centered life, they will be revealed to you. They may be:

1. Business cards and phone numbers
2. Jewelry, gifts, or other presents
3. Pornographic magazines, movies, and videos
4. R-rated movies and some PG-13 as well
5. Past feelings of anger, resentment, or bitterness
6. Pride
7. Selfishness
8. Unrealistic expectation of sexual relations within marriage
9. Unhealthy friends
10. Romance novels
11. Soap operas
12. Inappropriate materials obtained through the Internet
13. Computer chat lines
14. Computer pornography
15. Flirting with the opposite sex
16. Not being able to tell someone No!
17. Always trying to be Mr. Nice Guy or Ms. Nice Gal
18. Sexually explicit movies, provocative or suggestive TV shows

Please write some of the jars of grain that you would like to surrender.

1. _____

2. _____

3. _____

4. _____

It's important that we lay aside each jar of grain and surrender it to God. Alma said, *"Yea, I say unto you come and fear not, and lay aside every sin, which easily doth beset you, which doth bind you down to destruction, yea, come and go forth, and show unto your God that ye are willing to repent of your sins and enter into a covenant with him to keep his commandments."* (Alma 7:15)

THE PARABLE OF THE SMILING PUMPKIN

A young lady wanted to attend a girl's choice dance at the high school. The big question was how should she ask the young man she wanted to take.

Finally, after much thought, she decided on a unique way. She bought a large pumpkin and carefully cut a hole in the bottom. Inside the hole she inserted the wrapped invitation. She carefully covered the hole and colored the markings with orange paint. The young man would have to search inside the pumpkin for the hidden message. Then, if he wanted to accept her invitation, he was to carve a smiling face on the pumpkin and return it to the doorstep of the girl's home. If he couldn't go, he was to carve a frowning face on the pumpkin and return it.

Three days passed and there was no pumpkin delivered. Did someone steal the pumpkin off the front porch before he found it? Did he not find the invitation inside the pumpkin? Does he not know how to carve a pumpkin? Does he need some help in drawing a pattern? Why hadn't the pumpkin been delivered?

Finally, after three days, the pumpkin was on the doorstep with a burning candle inside. The light flickered in the darkness. The face on the pumpkin was not a happy face. The young man included a handwritten note; he had already been asked by someone else and had accepted. He had no other choice but to return the pumpkin with a frowning face.

The young lady felt very sad. She shed a few tears. He had told her no.

Did he still like her? Did he still want to talk with her when he saw her at school? Did he still want to be a friend? The answer was yes to these questions, but he had already promised someone else. Even though she could see why he could not go, it was still not easy to accept. All of that planning, working, and sneaking to the door to drop off the pumpkin and still no date for the dance.

With less enthusiasm than before, she bought another pumpkin and decided on another young man to invite. This was very scary. What if he couldn't go? What would she say to her friends if she was turned down by two young men? One "no" was bad enough, but what about two?

She made a small hole in the bottom of another pumpkin and inserted another invitation inside the hole, then used orange paint to cover the markings. She delivered the pumpkin to a different house. One day passed and there was no sign of the pumpkin. Could the same thing happen again?

The next day early in the afternoon, a pumpkin arrived at the doorstep of this young lady's house. When the young lady returned from school, she saw the pumpkin and her face broke into a great big smile. It was going to be a fun night.

In life we can't control whether someone carves a smile or a frown on our pumpkin. We can't control what someone else decides to do. But we can control how we respond to the carving. It's okay to feel sad. It's okay to feel hurt. It's okay to feel rejected, but it's not okay to do nothing about it or to choose a compulsive sexual behavior to cover up the feeling that we don't like to feel.

Once we feel those feelings, we should talk about them with someone we trust—perhaps Dad, Mom, sister, brother, spouse, or trusted friend. They can help us get through the hard times. In moments like these, we can also pray to Heavenly Father and say, "Heavenly Father, I feel very sad tonight. I feel hurt that this boy couldn't go to the dance. Help me, Father, to realize that I'm still one of Thy daughters and that Thou lovest me whether I go to the dance or not. Please help me, Father, to feel Thy love. Help me as I read the scriptures tonight that I might know how important I am. I know that I am one of Thy daughters and that Thou hearest my prayers."

What about the smiling face on the pumpkin? Should that be treated any differently? "Heavenly Father, I'm so grateful that this young man can go to the dance. Help me, Father, to be humble and to be grateful for life. Help me, Father, to appreciate the moments of joy. As I read the scriptures tonight, help me to understand more about humility and gratitude."

God sent us to earth to get a body and to have experiences that would help us grow and progress. There will be *many times* in life when someone carves a frown on our pumpkins. There will be *some times* in life when someone carves a smile. Can we still smile when someone carves a frown?

Yes, as we turn to Heavenly Father—we can smile. The smile may not come the same day, but the light within us, the light of Christ, will glow and eventually turn that frown upside down and smile it away.

List several ways you can deal with negative emotions in a Christ-centered way.

1. _____

_____

_____

2. _____

_____

_____

3. _____

_____

_____

4. _____

_____

_____

_____

7

Using Divine Relationships to Fill Emotional Needs

Begin to use your relationship with Heavenly Father and Jesus Christ to fill your emotional needs and to replace trigger points. Plan your week in advance with Christ-centered choices that are positive replacements for your trigger points.

And now, my sons, remember, remember that it is upon the rock of our Redeemer, who is Christ, the Son of God, that ye must build your foundation; that when the devil shall send forth his mighty winds, yea, his shafts in the whirlwind, yea, when all his hail and his mighty storm shall beat upon you, it shall have no power over you to drag you down to the gulf of misery and endless wo, because of the rock upon which ye are built, which is a sure foundation, a foundation whereon if men build they cannot fall. (Helaman 5:12)

CHRIST-CENTERED CHOICES

By making Christ-centered choices (such as sincere prayer, searching the scriptures, and meaningful unassigned service to glorify God) you are building a solid foundation.

List some Christ-centered choices you can make in the time periods shown when you begin to feel out-of-balanced emotions. For example, when you feel lonely, what's a Christ-centered choice you can make in the next one minute so you won't feel lonely? What's a Christ-centered choice you can make in the next hour? What's a Christ-centered choice you can make in the next twenty-four hours?

One Minute Choices

1. Call a trusted friend.

2. _____

3. _____

4. _____

5. _____

One Hour Choices

1. Read the scriptures during my lunch hour.

2. _____

3. _____

4. _____

5. _____

Twenty-four Hour Choices

1. Write down the entire experience on paper. Get everything out. Write exactly how I feel. Afterwards, discard the paper.

2. _____

3. _____

4. _____

5. _____

Sincere Prayer

Prayer is another tool to help us draw on our Heavenly Father's power and to feel of Christ's love and avoid temptation. Alma said, *"Neither would they observe the performances of the church, to continue in prayer and supplication to God daily, that they might not enter into temptation."* (Alma 31:10) Elder Marion G. Romney emphasized the importance of prayer when he wrote: "No one ever reaches . . . perfection except those who are guided to it by Him who is perfect. And guidance from Him is to be had only through prayer." (*Improvement Era*, April, 1966, p. 275.)

Prayer is a Christ-centered choice that allows us to feel the whisperings of the Spirit. President Harold B. Lee counseled:

> The most important thing you can do is to learn to talk to God. Talk to Him as you would talk to your father, for He is your Father, and He wants you to talk to Him. He wants you to cultivate ears to listen, when He gives you the impressions of the Spirit to

tell you what to do. If you learn to give heed to the sudden ideas which come to your minds, you will find those things coming through in the very hour of your need. If you will cultivate an ear to hear these promptings, you will have learned to walk by the Spirit of revelation. ("Pres. Lee Gives Solemn Witness," *Church News*, 3 March, 1973, p. 3)

As we pray and learn to walk by the Spirit we can become our best selves. President Monson used President Benson's statement on prayer at the opening of the April 1991 General Conference:

> Our Heavenly Father is always near . . . . Thank God we can reach out and tap that unseen power, without which no man can do his best."
> (Message delivered to temple workers and church employees at Sao Paulo, Brazil, 20 November, 1982. (*Ensign*, May 1991, p. 5)

Prayer is a Christ-centered choice that we can use to deal positively with our out-of-balance emotions. The first step is to pray. The next step, which follows naturally, is to love to pray. We should surrender out-of-balance emotions and afflictions to God through prayer. The prophet Zenos, as quoted in Alma 33:11 said, "*I will cry unto thee in all mine afflictions, for in thee is my joy; for thou hast turned thy judgments away from me, because of thy Son.*"

When our emotions are starting to get out of balance, we only have a few seconds or minutes to make a Christ-centered choice. If the choice is not made quickly, the emotion picks up speed and can get out of control. The longer the out-of-balance emotion goes unchecked, the more difficult it is to stop. Every small snowball, if it keeps rolling and gathering more snow, may eventually become an avalanche. With Christ's help you can surrender each out-of-balance emotional snowball, and stop its rolling while it is small. If we fail to surrender the snowballs, it won't be long before we have to deal with an avalanche.

In Helaman 4:26 we read, "*And thus had they fallen into this great transgression; yea, thus had they become weak, because of their transgression, in the space of not many years.*"

List ways you can improve your personal prayers to make them more meaningful.

1. Spend a few minutes before the prayer thinking about all of the good things in life. Also, reflect on the challenges that have helped you to grow.

2. _____

3. _____

4. _____

5. _____

Searching the Scriptures
Reading the scriptures focuses our attention on Christ and provides healing of our out-of-balance emotions. We can avoid temptations and the fiery darts of the adversary as we search the scriptures and hold fast to them.

Nephi explained to his brothers the meaning of the rod of iron: "*And I said unto them that it was the word of God; and whoso would hearken unto the word of God, and would hold fast unto it, they would never perish; neither could the temptations and the fiery darts of the adversary overpower them unto blindness, to lead them away to destruction.*" (1 Nephi 15:24)

The following verses from Hymn 277 teach the power of the scriptures in our lives. Read carefully the words in verse three.

As I Search the Holy Scriptures

As I search the holy scriptures,
Loving Father of mankind.
May my heart be blessed with wisdom,
And may knowledge fill my mind.

As I search the holy scriptures,
Touch my spirit, Lord, I pray.
May life's mysteries be unfolded,
As I study day by day.

As I search the holy scriptures,
May thy mercy be revealed.
Soothe my troubled heart and spirit;
May my unseen wounds be healed.

As I search the holy scriptures
Help me ponder and obey.
In thy word is life eternal;
May thy light show me the way.

I want to repeat the third verse: "As I search the holy scriptures, May thy mercy be revealed. Soothe my troubled heart and spirit; May my unseen wounds be healed." Jesus Christ can heal our unseen emotional wounds as we turn to Him. Reading the scriptures is a Christ-centered choice. The first step is to read the scriptures. The next step, which follows naturally, is to love the scriptures.

As you study the scriptures, apply them to you. This will make them more meaningful. If I were working to overcome inappropriate thoughts, I would change 1 Nephi 3:7 to say. *"And it came to pass that I, [Rod], said unto my father* [Nephi's father was the prophet]: *I will go and do the things which the Lord hath commanded, for I know that the Lord giveth no commandments* [such as to avoid inappropriate thoughts] *unto [Rod], save he shall prepare a way for [Rod] that he may accomplish the thing which he commandeth* [him]." What a wonderful promise. The Lord doesn't give us any commandment without providing for us a way to accomplish the commandment. It took Nephi three tries to accomplish the Lord's commandment to get the plates of brass. Nephi kept trying. The Lord provided a way. As we keep trying, He will do the same for us.

List ways you can improve your scripture study to make the words of Christ come alive in your life.

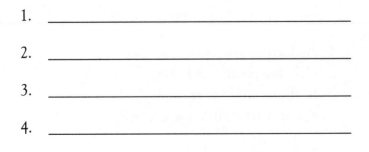

1. _____

2. _____

3. _____

4. _____

As we study the scriptures, we are making Christ-centered choices that will help us to deal positively with our emotional out-of-balance trigger points. Elder Dallin H. Oaks said, "In all of this, we should remember King Benjamin's caution to '*see that all these things are done in wisdom and order; for it is not requisite that a man should run faster than he has strength*'" (Mosiah 4:27). And then Elder Oaks added, "I think of that inspired teaching whenever I feel inadequate, frustrated, or depressed." (*Ensign*, November, 1993 p. 75)

Reading the scriptures is a Christ-centered choice that helps us to deal in a positive way with feelings of inadequacy, frustration, or depression.

Meaningful Unassigned Service to Glorify God

Another positive way to avoid giving trigger points attention or power in our lives is to provide meaningful, unassigned service to glorify God. You can do this by helping parents, brothers, sisters, spouse, friends, neighbors, or strangers without being asked. Do it without looking for anything in return. The first step is to do unassigned service. The next step, that seems to follow naturally, is to love doing unassigned service.

After you finish, thank Heavenly Father, through prayer, for the opportunity to help one of His sons or daughters. Providing meaningful, unassigned service is a Christ-centered choice that builds our spiritual bodies and allows us to resist Satan.

Elder M. Russell Ballard said, "If you will pay more attention to your spiritual self, which is eternal, than to your mortal self, which is temporary, you can always resist the temptations of Satan and conquer his efforts to take you into his power." (*Ensign*, May 1993, p. 7)

List ways you can give meaningful, unassigned service to glorify God.

1. Do something for your parents or other relatives that they are not expecting.

2. _____

3. _____

4. _____

5. _____

As children of God we have been blessed with His spiritual power. This power can be used to resist Satan. President George Q. Cannon testified that every man has power enough to resist Satan. "The Lord our God has sent us here to get experience in these things so that we may know the good from the evil and be able to close our hearts against the evil . . . It is true that some have greater power of resistance than others, but everyone has the power to close his heart against doubt, against darkness, against unbelief, against depression, against anger, against hatred, against jealousy, against malice, against envy. God has given this power unto all of us, and we can gain still greater power by calling upon Him for that which we lack. If it were not so, how could we be condemned for giving way to wrong influences?" (Doctrine and Covenants Student Manual, p. 161)

As we identify Christ-centered choices that deal positively with our trigger points, we avoid the river of filthiness in the world. In Lehi's vision he identified the river of water which flowed next to the rod of iron as filthiness.

Nephi said his father Lehi was so focused on other things (Christ-centered choices) that the filthiness of the water did not bother Him. *"And I said unto them that the water which my father saw was filthiness; and so much was his mind swallowed up in other things that he beheld not the filthiness of the water."* (1 Nephi 15:27)

TRIGGER POINTS AND SOLUTIONS

Each day most of us spend time planning our calendar of events. Why not plan our emotional schedules in advance? For example, if we know that it's going to be a stressful week, why not schedule some time for relaxation. If a potential customer is going to let us know Wednesday whether we received the contract, plan ahead emotionally in case the contract goes to a competitor. Once we know our trigger points, the next step is to plan ahead, whenever possible, so we are emotionally ready and in balance to deal with them.

Here is a list of some trigger points and a solution that a compulsive sexual person found to deal positively with the trigger point.

Trigger: Away from home on a business trip—alone in a motel room.

Solution: Stay at a bed and breakfast.

Trigger: When I initiate sex with my wife and she is not interested, I feel rejected.

Solution: I say to my wife, "Honey, I need to talk about how I feel right now. Is that okay? I feel rejected. I feel unloved. I'm not asking you to change anything, but I need to tell you how I feel." I am responsible for how I feel; my wife is not responsible for my emotions. Sharing my feelings will give my wife an opportunity to put her arms around me and say, "I didn't mean to have you feel this way. I love you and care about you, but physically, I'm just not up to having sex with you tonight." If she doesn't say these things, I'm still responsible for my own emotions.

Trigger: When I see a girl outside wearing short shorts or a tank top I have difficulty keeping my thoughts in line.

Solution: When I see a girl in shorts or a tank top, I choose to think, "Father in Heaven, there is one of Thy daughters. Help me to respect her in my thoughts and treat her as one of Thy daughters. May Thou bless her and may she find peace in Thee."

Trigger: This is going to be a stressful week.

Solution: When I know in advance that a week is going to be stressful, I will plan my emotional week and look for ways to deal with stress in a positive way. Perhaps two ten-minute walks around the block each day will help. At home I can sit and pet my dog. I can take one of my children over to the ice cream store. I can listen to some uplifting and relaxing music. I can find a child's coloring book and color several drawings.

Trigger: I've always been so independent. I don't want to ask for help from anyone.

Solution: I asked my bishop for a blessing to specifically help me to deal with this compulsive sexual behavior.

Trigger: I am so bored. There's nothing to do.

Solution: Plan each day. Call friends that I trust and get something set up. Give a family member some special time today.

Trigger: Each time I stop to get gas, I can see the pornographic magazines behind the counter.

Solution: I buy gas from a different gas station that doesn't sell pornography, although it's several blocks out of my way.

Trigger: Negative things always happen to me. I get so sick and tired of being the person who always gets dumped on.

Solution: I need to make sure that I'm not allowing people to dump on me. I am a worthy, capable person. I have to protect myself. I need to take responsibility for how I feel and be willing to share those feelings, when appropriate, with others. Today I'm going to go out of my way and do something for someone else. I want to help someone because of the love I have for Jesus Christ.

Trigger: There is nothing exciting going on. Is this all there is to life?

Solution: Accept life as it is. I've been involved in an unreal world of fantasy and make believe. Because I've been involved with this lifestyle for so long, I think it is real. However, I'm never satisfied. I'm always looking for more. It will take time to notice the flowers, the trees, a small child, and all of God's other beautiful creations. One of the exciting things about real life is to achieve balance.

Trigger: I'm so bored I have nothing to do.

Solution: I'm going downstairs to lift weights.

Trigger: My friends want to go see an R-rated movie.

Solution: I'm going to stay home tonight and read a good book.

Trigger: I see a lingerie ad in the newspaper and have trouble controlling my thoughts.

Solution: When I see this ad I choose to pray: "Heavenly Father, help me to think of this model as one of Thy daughters. May I respect her womanhood. May I recognize that she has feelings and emotions."

Trigger: I am so angry right now.

Solution: If it's appropriate, go to the person and say, "I need to talk about how I feel. Right now I am very angry. I feel angry. I am very upset."

Trigger: I'm so mad at him I want to punch his lights out.

Solution: It wasn't appropriate to talk to him right then, so I wrote him a letter and told him exactly how I felt. I told him how angry I was at him for the way he made me feel. I never mailed the letter, instead I tore it up piece by piece until there was nothing left. I never said a word to the person, but that letter-writing experience made me feel like a new person. I can honestly say that the anger I once felt toward the person is now gone.

Trigger: No one seems to care about me or what I need.

Solution: I stopped at a rest home on the way home from work. I read to an elderly person. I now feel needed. It took about thirty minutes of my time. My out-of-balance emotion is gone for now.

Trigger: I feel so guilty when I go to church.

Solution: I went to church and kept reminding myself that the Church is for the sinners, and that all of us are sinners. No one but Christ is perfect. I also reminded myself that Christ loves me unconditionally. I need to understand godly sorrow. I need to feel sorrow because I have violated one of God's laws. Godly sorrow draws me closer to Christ and motivates me to repent. When I keep telling myself I am no good, this thinking process takes me from Christ.

Trigger: I'm tired. When I get tired, it's easy for my thoughts to start to wander.

Solution: I eat a quick lunch and then sleep in my car for fifteen minutes. I have a wind up alarm clock. It's great! I feel refreshed. It's like getting two days out of one.

Trigger: I'm so hungry I can't stand it.

Solution: I have a can of fruit juice in the fridge at work. I also keep a box of crackers in my desk. Late in the afternoon, I have a snack.

Trigger: I get so stressed out at work. When I get home, I can't get my mind to relax.

Solution: I bought a dog for my kids. They've always wanted one, but I didn't want the hassle. I now spend about ten minutes, when I get home, playing with my dog. This makes me feel relaxed and helps me to unwind.

Trigger: It seems like I'm bored a lot of the time around the house. There's nothing that's exciting or that I look forward to.

Solution: I started piano lessons again. It doesn't matter if I ever play in public. I'm enjoying my time practicing and performing for my family. After several weeks of practice, I can play "Jingle Bells" without any mistakes.

Trigger: Life sometimes is boring no matter what I do. Satan whispers to me to go dancing since dancing is really not a sin.

Solution: I make myself realize that dancing with other women can easily lead to more serious transgressions, so I do not go where couples dance without my wife being present.

Trigger: I was mad at the person at the city offices. He was just plain rude and thought he was king of the hill. I tried to explain my viewpoint, but he wouldn't listen.

Solution: I wrote a letter to his boss and told him how I felt I was treated.

Trigger: I'm away from home on a business trip with a lot of free time in the evenings.

Solution: I sought to have dinner with those around me to occupy my evening hours so I would be too tired for any activities afterward. I tried to occupy my mind with positive thoughts by watching a good movie. I called my wife before midnight; I sought out good friends and relatives to cut down on my idle time; I took a long walk or jogged after dinner; I engage strangers only of the same sex in the lobby and initiate long conversations. I avoid motels with adjourning bars, lounges, or dance halls since dancing was always my preferred method of contacting women.

Trigger: My job required me to do so much traveling, I found it impossible to change my compulsive behavior.

Solution: I loved my work, but I changed to a job where I was home all my non-working hours. My home was next door to the office, so my wife always knew where to find me.

Trigger: I see ladies in shorts and tight blouses or I see ads in the newspaper advertising bras.

Solution: I immediately change my thoughts to the Savior in the Garden of Gethsemane and remember all the pain and suffering He voluntarily underwent for me personally, a sinner, and try to feel His unconditional love for me. I also remember that all of us, including the women in the ads, are children of God with feelings and emotions. They were formed like they are for many reasons, such as: procreation, thought, movement, creativity, beauty, digestion, etc.

Trigger: Since coming back from my mission, I have no specific church assignment and I slowed down or quit my scripture reading.

Solution: I realize Satan sees this as his big opportunity to make me his, so I set new goals for scripture reading and spend more time fulfilling church assignments. I also asked the bishop to put me to work.

Trigger: I do something I know to be contrary to God's commandments, but I say to myself it's not that serious.

Solution: I know one sinful act can and will lead to another, so I go to a support group meeting. For me, this clears my thinking and helps me to realize that I must continually be on guard or I could stumble.

Trigger: Things constantly change. I don't deal well with change.

Solution: The seasons change from spring to summer and from fall to winter. People make changes. Some changes are for the good and some are for the bad. Businesses change. Relationships with people change. Change is part of life. I must accept change and only concern myself with those things that I have control over.

Trigger: It's been sixty days and I haven't had a problem. It hasn't been all that hard.

Solution: I need to stay humble and remind myself that I have additional power and strength as I surrender my out-of-balance emotions to my Heavenly Father. With God's help I can continue to progress. If I get over-confident, I'm setting myself up for a fall.

Trigger: I'm on a business trip and see an attractive lady. I make eye contact with her. My next thought is, I want to talk with her and see what happens. I just want to be friendly; I'm not going to do anything.

Solution: It's okay to recognize another human being's beauty. God created all of us; but I know I need to avoid talking with attractive women with the intent to see what happens. I need to see women as human beings and associate with them on a normal level instead of seeing them as a sex object. Also, I need to wear my wedding band always.

How can I deal with my trigger points? Each person has his own set of trigger points. I suggest you list your trigger points. You know your trigger points better than anyone else. You are an expert on your trigger points.

After you have listed your trigger points, write down your positive solution on how you can deal with each one.

Trigger:_____

_____

_____

Solution: _____

_____

_____

_____

_____

Trigger:_____

_____

_____

Solution: _____

_____

_____

_____

_____

Trigger:_____

_____

_____

Solution: _____

_____

_____

_____

_____

The Real Target

The real target is the trigger point. A compulsive sexual behavior is the result of trigger points that were not dealt with in a positive, Christ-centered way. Sometimes people have said to me, "Oh, if I could just give up this compulsive sexual behavior, I would be so happy." I respond that the real target is your trigger point, not the compulsive sexual behavior. As you surrender your trigger points to God and Christ, the compulsive sexual behavior will be eliminated. You cannot serve the trigger point with one hand and expect to serve God and Christ with the other hand. Let go of the trigger points, surrender them, and grab hold with both hands to the outstretched arms of the Savior. As you do so, Christ will take away the power your trigger points have over you. He has promised us, *"Then will I make weak things become strong unto them."* (Ether 12:27) In Christ we can find peace.

Where Can I Turn for Peace?

Where can I turn for peace? Where is my solace.
When other sources cease to make me whole?
When with a wounded heart, anger or malice,
I draw myself apart, Searching my soul?

Where, when my aching grows,
Where, when I languish,
Where, in my need to know, where can I run?
Where is the quiet hand to calm my anguish?
Who, who can understand? He, only One.

He answers privately, Reaches my reaching
In my Gethsemane, Savior and Friend.
Gentle the peace he finds for my beseeching.
Constant he is and kind, Love without end.
(Hymn 129, Text written by Emma Lou Thayne)

Each time a person goes without the drug of lust for a day, two days, or a week, it's a miracle. To me it's just as powerful a miracle as feeding the five thousand with five loaves of bread and two fishes. You came into this world as another miracle—birth is a miracle. When you were born you started a new life in mortality. Now you are ready to begin another new life—a Christ-centered life. Yes, another miracle. Keep surrendering your trigger points to God through prayer. As you do, you will be the next miracle.

8

Christ Has the Power to Heal Our Weaknesses

Know that God and Christ love us unconditionally even with our weaknesses. As we turn to Christ, He will make our weaknesses become strengths.

> And if men come unto me I will show unto them their weakness. I give unto men weakness that they may be humble; and my grace is sufficient for all men that humble themselves before me; for if they humble themselves before me, and have faith in me, then will I make weak things become strong unto them. (Ether 12:27)

HE CAN HEAL OUR WEAKNESSES

President Benson quoted this scripture in his First Presidency Message and said, "*It matters not what is our lack or our weakness or our insufficiency. His gifts and power are sufficient to overcome them all. (Ensign, October 1989, p. 4)*

Let's review the key points made in Ether 12:27.

- First, *"Come unto me."*
- Second, *"I will show unto them their weakness."*
- Third, *"I give unto men weakness that they may be humble."*
- Fourth, *"My grace is sufficient for all men that humble themselves before me."*
- Fifth, *"Have Faith in me."*
- Sixth, *"Then will I make weak things become strong unto them."*

In the first step Christ says, *"Come unto me."* We do this by doing the little things I previously mentioned: daily prayer, reading the scriptures, unassigned service.

We often don't even realize that these little things do make a big difference over time. We don't even realize that we are building a Christlike life.

President Benson said, "Day by day they move closer to the Lord, little realizing they are building a godlike life. They live quiet lives of goodness, service, and commitment. They are like the Lamanites, who the Lord said, 'Were baptized with fire and with the Holy Ghost, and they knew it not.'" (*Ensign*, October 1989, p. 5)

As we do the little things, Christ promises us step two: *Christ will show us our weakness.* Isn't it refreshing to know that Christ will show us our weakness? We no longer have to rely on our spouse to tell us our weakness or our teenage children. Christ will show us our weakness. When someone who is perfect tells us our weakness, it's a lot easier to accept.

Now, after we know our weakness, what is the next step? Step three, *be humble.* How can we be humble? By completely confessing and repenting of our sins. As we confess our sins with a broken heart and a contrite spirit to our bishop, we will be blessed with humility. Humility allows us to rely on Christ.

In humility, knowing our weakness, step four begins. *"My grace is sufficient for all men that humble themselves before me."* This is a promise. His grace is sufficient. He will carry the load. He will carry the burden. He will carry the sin. His grace will allow mercy to operate and satisfy justice.

In order for His grace to work in our lives we need to have faith in Him. Step five, *Have faith in me*. It doesn't say faith in yourself. It doesn't say faith in your own abilities. Even though we need to recognize our strengths and abilities we need to have faith in Him and not try to save ourselves.

How can we show faith in Christ? We can surrender our weakness to Him instead of trying to get rid of the weakness by ourselves. Just like a child who says, "I want to do it myself!" At times we want to do everything by ourselves, but we can't save ourselves. Only when we surrender to the power of Christ in our lives comes the good news, that which we have prayed for, fasted for, and hoped for. It is found in step six, *"Then will I make weak things become strong unto them."*

THE SURRENDER PROCESS

Let's say that by going through this six-step process we learn from Christ that anger is one of our weaknesses. How do we overcome our anger? How do we allow Christ to remove it from us? In step one we turn to Christ by doing the little things—day in and day out—even when we don't feel like it.

In Step two Christ told us He would show us our weaknesses. He didn't say He would tell us our parent's weaknesses or our neighbors', but only our own. After Christ tells us our weakness, we admit that we have the weakness and we accept responsibility for it. We don't blame others. We don't blame our parents. We don't blame our neighbors. We accept it.

In step three we recognize that we must be humble and rely on Christ in order to give up the anger. In step four we recognize that Christ's grace covers everything including anger if we are humble and turn to Him. In step five we begin to exercise faith in Christ and surrender our weaknesses to God. How do we do this? We surrender. That's right. We give our weakness of anger to God. He's perfect and He knows how to deal with anger in a positive way.

We surrender by saying whenever we feel angry, "Heavenly Father, right now I am so very angry. I am so upset. I need Thy strength. Help me, Father, to surrender this horrible experience to Thee. Help me, Father, to stop replaying the scene over and over again in my mind. Help me replace this experience with a peaceful experience." When the emotions are still high, we may have to surrender many times. We may have to give a surrender prayer a hundred times in one day.

Focus on the Feeling, not the Actions

Other suggestions may help. First, we may, when it's appropriate, talk to the person involved. In these situations we should only talk about how we feel, not about what the other person may have said or done. In other words instead of saying, "When you do that I get so mad."

say something like, "I feel very angry right now because of the way that was said. I feel angry."

The emphasis is on how *you* feel, not what the other person did. We focus on the feelings, not on the other person's actions.

Another positive way to deal with anger is to write a letter to the person which you never mail. You write down the experience, the feelings, the anger—then tear up the letter.

In far too many situations, we allow people we are angry with to live in our heads "rent free." That's right. We replay situations over and over again and begin to worship the false god of anger instead of the true and living God.

We cannot hold onto the anger and still expect to worship God. By surrendering to God, we are worshiping Him again. On bended knees we are giving up the anger. We gain victory by surrendering. This method of surrender works as we apply it to any weakness.

As we surrender to Christ our weaknesses, He can remove them. We cannot do it ourselves. *We were not sent to earth to see how much we could do alone, but rather to see how much we could do with Christ's help.*

The final step—step six—is the miracle. Christ will make our weak things become strong. Perhaps we have not had as much success as we would like because we have tried to do it all by ourselves and have not used the power of Christ. *Positive change is made through progressive Christ-centered steps, not one event or occurrence.* President Benson said, "Becoming Christlike is a lifetime pursuit and very often involves growth and change that is slow, almost imperceptible." (*Ensign,* October 1989, p. 5)

What are some positive steps you have taken in the last three weeks to surrender your compulsive sexual behavior? Give yourself credit for every little step even though it may seem small. Small, consistent steps in the right direction will eventually put us in the footsteps of Christ.

1. _____

_____

2. _____

_____

3. _____

_____

4. _____

_____

5. _____

_____

His Hand Is Extended

We need to separate who we are from what we have done. We are sons or daughters of the living God. He loves us unconditionally. A few years ago some special friends of mine stopped by to talk, as they did on a regular basis. After our little talks we would have a treat. I learned very quickly that they didn't come for the talks, or even for the treats, but for the attention I gave them. Their names were Jennie, Jacob, and Sam. Sam was six, Jennie was four, and Jacob was two-and-a-half. They are the youngest of ten children.

One time after our talk and treat, Jennie said, "You like

me, don't you." I said "Jennie, I love you!" Pointing to her brothers, she said, "Do you love Jacob?" "Yes, I love Jacob!" "Do you love Sam?" "Yes, I love Sam!" Then she named all her other brothers and sisters, then went on to her parents. "Do you love my Mommy?"

"Yes, I love your Mommy!" "Do you love my Daddy?" "Yes, I love your Daddy!"

And then with those inquisitive eyes of a four-year-old she asked, "Do you love yourself?" I responded the same way I had to the other questions; she had conditioned me. But it made me think about myself for a few days after that. I decided I sometimes do not like the things I say. I sometimes do not like the things I do. I do not like the way I pout around the house sometimes, but I do love myself all the time. I love who I am. There is a difference between who we are and what we do.

Divine Nature

We are all sons and daughters of God and have been given a divine nature. We can hate the things we do, but we can still love ourselves. Sometimes we beat ourselves up too much. Godly sorrow brings appropriate guilt; it brings us to our knees to repent and draws us closer to Jesus Christ.

Worldly sorrow produces inappropriate guilt and self-hate and takes us further from Christ. Christ wants us to have godly sorrow that will turn us to Him and allow us to know that He is with us.

In the topical guide there is *one full column* of references under the heading "Commandments of God." That's a lot of references on how we should live. But what should we do if we violate one of God's commandments? We should follow the steps of repentance and ask for forgiveness. In the topical guide *one and a half columns* appear under the heading of "Forgiveness." The Lord and his prophets apparently spent more time teaching repentance and forgiveness than they did on repeating the commandments.

TEMPTATION IS REAL

Although you may have repented, Satan will continue to tempt you. No matter how righteously we are living, he never lets up on any of us. Brigham Young said:

> Do not suppose that we shall ever in the flesh be free from temptations to sin. Some suppose that they can in the flesh be sanctified body and spirit and become so pure that they will never again feel the effects of the power of the adversary of truth. Were it possible for a person to attain to the degree of perfection in the flesh, he could not die neither remain in a world where sin predominates. Sin has entered into the world, and death by sin. I think we shall more or less feel the effects of sin so long as we live, and finally have to pass the ordeals of death. (*Journal of Discourses*, 10:173)

The Savior loves us and wants us to become our best selves. He wants to help if we will but turn to Him! Although we will always be tempted, by surrendering our out-of-balance emotions to Christ's power, we can withstand the temptations.

The Savior said:

I am come a light into the world. (John 12:46)

Draw near unto me and I will draw near unto you. (D&C 88:63)

I will be on your right hand and on your left. (D&C 84:88)

I will be merciful unto your weakness. (D&C 38:14)

Thy sins are forgiven thee. (Enos 1:5)

Behold, and lo, I will come quickly, and receive you unto myself. (D&C 88:126)

As you ponder these scriptures, think of some specific things you can do to withstand Satan's temptations.

1. _____
   _____

2. _____
   _____

3. _____
   _____

4. _____
   _____

5. _____
   _____

9

Prepare Every Needful Thing

———♦———

Fast at least monthly and establish and commit to a regular physical exercise program.

Organize yourselves; prepare every needful thing; and establish a house, even a house of prayer, a house of fasting, a house of faith, a house of learning, a house of glory, a house of order, a house of God; That your incomings may be in the name of the Lord; that your outgoings may be in the name of the Lord; that all your salutations may be in the name of the Lord, with uplifted hands unto the Most High. (D&C 88:119–120)

EXERCISE

Exercise is a way to keep the temporal body in shape. The spirit is designed to control the body. As we keep spiritually and physically fit, we will have power from on high to control our appetites, passions, and desires.

You should establish an exercise program that allows you to exercise at least twenty to thirty minutes, four to five times each week. Some of the advantages of exercise include the following:

1. Increased concentration at school or work
2. Reduced stress and tension
3. Increased muscle tone so you won't tire as easily
4. Improved heart and other bodily functions
5. During exercise you can plan your day, ponder difficult situations that you may be experiencing, and memorize thoughts and scriptures.

Exercise programs may include:

Jogging	Basketball	Handball
Bicycling	Swimming	Jumping rope
Tennis	Snowskiing	Aerobics
Waterskiing	Walking briskly	

I have chosen_____as my exercise activity and will spend twenty to thirty minutes at least four to five times each week exercising.

FASTING

Fasting also gives our spiritual bodies an increase of power. As we deprive our temporal bodies of food, we can focus more on our spiritual bodies.

Certain feelings, desires, or bad spirits will leave only through prayer and fasting.

When Jesus saw that the people came running together, he rebuked the foul spirit, saying unto him, Thou dumb and deaf spirit, I charge thee, come out of him, and enter no more into him. And the spirit cried, and rent him sore, and came out of him: and he was as one dead; insomuch that many said, He is dead. But Jesus took him by the hand, and lifted him up; and he arose. And when he was come into the house, his disciples asked him privately, Why could not we cast him out? And he said unto them, This kind can come forth by nothing, but by prayer and fasting. (Mark 9:25-29)

Exercise and fasting can help maintain the temporal body and keep it fit for the spiritual body.

Know ye not that ye are the temple of God, and that the Spirit of God dwelleth in you? If any man defile the temple of God, him shall God destroy; for the temple of God is holy, which temple ye are. (1 Corinthians 3:16–17)

What spiritual blessings have you received through fasting and maintaining a regular exercise program?

1. _____

_____

2. _____

_____

3. _____

_____

10

We Believe All Things

Keep trying and never give up hope.

Wherefore, ye must press forward with a steadfastness in Christ, having a perfect brightness of hope, and a love of God and of all men. Wherefore, if ye shall press forward, feasting upon the word of Christ, and endure to the end, behold, thus saith the Father: Ye shall have eternal life. (2 Nephi 31:20)

Elder Theodore M. Burton said:

How grateful we should be for a kind, wise, loving Savior who will help us overcome our faults, our mistakes, and our sins. He loves and understands us and is sympathetic to the fact that we face temptations.

In the Book of Mormon, King Benjamin explains one way we can show our gratitude to the Lord for his great mercy and his sacrifice for our sins; *"Behold, I tell you these things that ye may learn wisdom: that ye may learn that when ye are in the service of your fellow beings ye are only in the service of your God."* (Mosiah 2:17)

God's work and glory is to redeem His children. If we participate in redemptive service to others, we can, in some small measure, repay Him for His blessings.

God is merciful; He has provided a way for us to apply the principle of repentance in our lives and thus escape the bondage of pain, sorrow, suffering, and despair that comes from disobedience. After all is said and done, we are God's sons and daughters. And for those who understand its true meaning, repentance is a beautiful word and a marvelous refuge. (*Ensign*, August 1988, p. 9)

TRACK YOUR PROGRESS

At times you may feel that you are making very little progress. Keep a daily journal about how the Lord has blessed you and the progress you have made in surrendering this compulsive behavior. When you are discouraged, read your journal and you will see the little steps of progress you have made and you will remember the Lord's blessings.

Satan wants you to feel that your progress is so slow that you might as well give up. He wants you to think you don't have the power to change, but with Heavenly

Father and Christ's help you can and will continue to make progress.

President Benson said:

> We must be careful, as we seek to become more and more godlike, that we do not become discouraged and lose hope. Becoming Christlike is a lifetime pursuit and very often involves growth and change that is slow, almost imperceptible. The scriptures record remarkable accounts of men whose lives changed dramatically, in an instant, as it were: Alma the Younger, Paul on the road to Damascus, Enos praying far into the night, King Lamoni. Such astonishing examples of the power to change even those steeped in sin give confidence that the Atonement can reach even those deepest in despair.
>
> But we must be cautious as we discuss these remarkable examples.
>
> Though they are real and powerful, they are the exception more than the rule. For every Paul, for every Enos, and for every King Lamoni, there are hundreds and thousands of people who find the process of repentance much more subtle, much more imperceptible. Day by day they move closer to the Lord, little realizing they are building a godlike life.
>
> We must not lose hope. Hope is an anchor to the souls of men. Satan would have us cast away that anchor. In this way he can bring discouragement and surrender. But we must not lose hope. The Lord is pleased with every effort, even the tiny, daily ones in which we strive to be more like Him. Though we may

see that we have far to go on the road to perfection, we must not give up hope." (*Ensign*, October 1989, p. 5)

May you continue and not lose hope. As you apply the ten steps and draw unto Christ, you will find peace and draw nearer and nearer to your best self.

THE SOLUTION CREATED A NEW PROBLEM

Here is a fable that illustrates my next point.

There was once a businessman who left the city to travel through the countryside to his next appointment. As he traveled down a two-lane highway, he saw a chicken running next to his car. He was amazed. The chicken was running at forty miles per hour. The man pressed the accelerator to fifty; the chicken stayed with him. Then to sixty and the chicken was still neck to neck with the car. Finally, the chicken made a turn into a farmer's barnyard. The businessman pulled his car over and started talking to the farmer. He said, "I can't believe it. That chicken was doing sixty miles an hour and I notice that it has three legs. That's remarkable!"

The farmer said, "Yes, I know. You see, I like drumsticks, my wife likes drumsticks, and so does my son. If I kill one chicken, we only get two drumsticks. So, I thought I could solve this problem by breeding a chicken with three legs; so that's what I did." The businessman said, "That's fantastic. Is the taste any different?" The farmer said, "I don't know. I haven't caught one yet."

The three-legged chicken was a good idea, but the farmer couldn't make the catch. At times we come up with a good solution to improve our lives or to make something better only to find we can't catch or achieve the intended results; we are several steps behind the chicken and are not closing the gap.

POSITIVE CHANGE THROUGH PROGRESSIVE STEPS

Sometimes the gap between where we are today and where we want to be seems too wide to ever cross. Sometimes it's so discouraging *but positive change is made through progressive Christ-centered steps, not one event or occurrence, not one giant leap.* Change is slow and seldom easy. Why are we not more successful in making positive change? Perhaps we put too much trust in ourselves.

The fourth Article of Faith says, *"We believe that the first principles and ordinances of the Gospel are: first, Faith in the Lord Jesus Christ; second, Repentance; third, Baptism by immersion for the remission of sins; fourth, Laying on of hands for the gift of the Holy Ghost."* This Article of Faith states that the first principle of the gospel is "faith in the Lord Jesus Christ" —not faith in ourselves, but rather, faith in the Lord Jesus Christ.

Keeping the Faith

Sometimes the experiences we have in life cause us to lose our faith. At other times the experiences we have, although they are painful, strengthen our faith. Recently, *Parade* magazine asked this question to its subscribers: "Do you believe in God?" Some of the responses were published on October 15, 1995. An eighteen-year-old girl wrote:

> I was taught that God was the Almighty and was good, but the past few months have set me straight.

There is no God. At least not the God everyone is talking about. If He/She was real, then there wouldn't be so much disease, death, hurt and heartbreak in the world. In December, one of my friends lost her mother. In January, a friend was killed on his way to school. In April, a friend of the family lost his long battle with AIDS. And in May, one of my best friends also lost her mother. What God would do this to anyone?

A thirty-four-year-old lady responded differently:

I was seventeen when I left high school, depressed, and without direction. I found myself pregnant and married a man who essentially reaffirmed that I was not going to amount to much. I later divorced him and continued making monumentally lousy decisions. Then I met someone, now my best friend. He too is a parent. He began to tell me that I was worth something. He listened as I expressed my disgust with what I had done with my life. At times, I even personally attacked him. But his patience was unbelievable. Today, I am a student in a very competitive medical program and a much better parent. I owe all my success to my best friend, who has been there every step of the way. So what does this have to do with whether I believe in God? Who do you think my best friend is?

Here are two examples of people who had very painful experiences. In one example, the young lady lost her faith in God. In the other example, the lady had her faith in

God strengthened. What is the difference between these two individuals? Why was one individual's faith strengthened and the other individual's faith weakened?

One Slice at a Time

To maintain our faith in God during the trials and difficulties, we must continue to do the little things that produce faith and power. In 1982 some statistics were released on the quantity of meat an average person will consume in seventy years (Booklet, "Sparks from the Anvil," p. 9).

I suppose if I were to take an eight-year-old child and drive to a barnyard and say, "By the time you reach age seventy (that's as old as grandpa is), you will have eaten everything in this barnyard—the two calves over there, the twelve sheep in that corner, the fourteen cattle right in front of you; the twenty-three pigs over there in the mud, the thirty-five turkeys under the wood covering, those 330 chickens and finally the 770 fish in that pond. You will eat all those animals and fish by the time you are age seventy." He probably would not believe me.

However, if I said to the eight-year-old, "What did you have for lunch yesterday?" He might respond with "A hot dog." If I asked, "What are you going to have for lunch today?" His answer might be, "A ham sandwich." Meal by meal, day by day, we eat one slice of meat here for this meal and another slice of meat for that meal until finally, at age seventy, we have consumed a lot of meat.

By comparison, how much spiritual food will we consume by age seventy?

Beginning at age eight and keeping track up to age seventy, if a person fasted every fast Sunday, by age seventy he will have fasted for a total of two years.

Beginning at age twenty-one to age seventy, if a person attended the temple once each month for three hours each time, by age seventy he will have spent ninety-three days in the temple.

Beginning at age eight to age seventy if a person reads five pages in the Book of Mormon each day, he will read the Book of Mormon 3.4 times each year and by age seventy he will have read the book 213 times.

Beginning at age eight to age seventy, if a person prays every morning for one and a half minutes and every night for one and a half minutes, by age seventy, he will have prayed for a total of forty-seven days.

These little things we do each day build Christlike lives. President Benson said, "Becoming Christlike is a lifetime pursuit and very often involves growth and change that is slow, almost imperceptible." (*Ensign*, October 1989, p. 5)

As we strive to become more Christlike, at times we may become discouraged. At times we lose patience with ourselves. It's important that we are patient with ourselves and our weaknesses. How we treat ourselves is as important to the Savior as how we treat anyone else.

An unknown author wrote the following poem:

Patience

Patience is mankind's greatest virtue
or so the saying goes.
A gymnast must have said it
for a gymnast surely knows
that in this funny sport of ours,
discouragement runs high
and at times the very best
will find this virtue pass them by.
When hands are ripped and throbbing
when every muscle's sore,
can a gymnast still have patience
to limp back in for more?

When you've lost old moves you used to
do and progress seems so slow—
can you still have faith in better days
and not feel sad and low?
Can you admit you're frightened
and yet not give in to fear?
Can you conquer pain, frustration
and sometimes even tears?
When someone else does something
you've tried so hard to do,
can you really feel glad for them
and not just pity you?
If despite these tribulations
you can say "I won't give in,"
maybe someday you'll discover
it's now your turn to win!

It's important to be patient. We talk about being patient with our spouse, our children, our employer, our neighbor, but what about being patient with ourselves and our own weaknesses? What about saying, "It's okay to be where I am on my course to building a Christlike life. The important thing is that I'm going in the right direction, and as long as I'm headed in the right direction, I'll eventually get where I want to go."

The Gospel Was Restored in Progressive Steps

How long should it take to reach a point where our weaknesses don't overpower us? At times we talk about the gospel being restored as though it were done in a single event. We bear our testimonies and say "I know that the gospel was restored." That makes it sound as if it happened in one day, but it was actually restored in progressive steps over a period of many years. Here is a brief outline of the progressive steps of the Restoration.

1820: Prophet has first vision

1823: Prophet instructed by Angel Moroni

1824: Prophet instructed by Angel Moroni at Hill Cumorah

1825: Prophet instructed by Angel Moroni at Hill Cumorah

1826: Prophet instructed by Angel Moroni at Hill Cumorah

1827: Prophet obtains Book of Mormon plates from angel Moroni at Hill Cumorah

1828: Prophet begins translation of the Book of Mormon

1829: Aaronic Priesthood restored by John the Baptist

1829: Melchizedek Priesthood restored by Peter, James, and John

1830: The Church is officially organized

1830: Book of Mormon is made available to the public

1832: Revelation on the three degrees of glory received (Section 76)

1833: Revelation on the Word of Wisdom received (Section 89)

1836: Section 110 of Doctrine and Covenants received. Moses restores the keys of the gathering of Israel; Elias restores the keys of the dispensation of the gospel of Abraham; Elijah restores the keys of fullness of the priesthood sealing power

1839: While a prisoner, Prophet receives D&C sections 121, 122, and 123.

1841: Prophet performs first eternal marriage sealing.

1843: Prophet is sealed to his wife Emma for time and eternity

1843: Revelation of celestial marriage recorded (D&C 132)

(Dates and events taken from "Highlights in the Prophet's Life," *Ensign*, June 1994.)

From the first vision in 1820 to the last revelation in 1843, twenty-three years had lapsed. During those twenty-three years, there was great progress made in restoring the gospel of Jesus Christ to the earth. During this twenty-three-year period the Prophet Joseph Smith had many struggles and difficulties. A son died within hours after birth. His twins lived for only three hours. His father died. A brother died. Another son died. There were countless false charges filed against him. Some of his closest friends left the church. He was imprisoned in Liberty Jail for months.

Is it any wonder the prophet begins D&C 121 by asking this question, *"O God, where art thou? And where is the pavilion that covereth thy hiding place?"* This is after the prophet had had many revelations, had felt the Spirit many times, but still had need to progress. He was still having experiences that would help him draw closer to Jesus Christ, if he chose to use them to do so.

Near the end of the prophet's life he said, *"I am going like a lamb to the slaughter; but I am calm as a summer's morning; I have a conscience void of offense towards God, and towards all men."* (D&C 135:4) Could the Prophet Joseph Smith have said, "I have a conscience void of offense towards God, and towards all men," while he was in Liberty Jail? Could he have made the same statement a year after the first vision? Could he have made that statement two years after the first vision? In my mind, the twenty-three years of refining were necessary in order for the Prophet to grow and progress and to be able to say that.

Isn't it necessary for all of God's children to be tempered and go through the refiner's fire in order for them to make positive change? Isn't it necessary to be refined through trials and challenges in order to grow and progress? Who is to say if it should take twenty-three days, twenty-three months, or twenty-three years to make positive changes?

If we consider the important 1978 Revelation received by President Spencer W. Kimball extending priesthood and temple blessings to all worthy male members of the Church, then it took a total of 158 years to restore the gospel. And we know that all things haven't been revealed even yet; there is still more to come (Ninth Article of Faith).

Just as the gospel of Jesus Christ was restored over a time line of important events, *positive change is accomplished through progressive Christ-centered steps*. It is not done through a single event or occurrence.

COMMON ELEMENTS OF RECOVERY

In this book I have told three dramatic, but true recovery stories. Even though each person's recovery varied slightly, there were some common threads that kept each person on a Christ-centered journey.

Each person:

- Confessed to a compulsive sexual thought pattern or lifestyle.

- Assumed full responsibility for the behavior.

- Stopped blaming others.

- Took total responsibility for setbacks and followed the complete repentance process.

- Through daily scripture study, prayer, kindness to others, and striving to live the commandments, their faith in the Atonement increased and they recognized that God loved them unconditionally, that the Atonement was for them, and that they could be made whole. They knew that they were loved by God even though they had committed serious sins.

- Identified out-of-balance emotional trigger points and used positive replacements that moved them closer to Jesus Christ.

- Realized that there is no such thing as controlled lust. Lust is lust.

- Recognized over time that anything associated with the compulsive sexual behavior had to be avoided. This list may include unhealthy friendships, names, phone numbers, magazines, videos, apartments, occupations, etc.

- In humility and in a spirit of repentance thanked God each day for another day of sobriety (freedom from the compulsive act).

- Recognized their dependence on God.

- Identified clearly their rational and irrational thought patterns and took responsibility for all irrational thought patterns.

- Recognized when a mistake was made and used the mistake to draw closer to Jesus Christ through complete repentance.

- Showed gratitude for repentance. After having fully repented, felt totally clean as though the sin had never occurred. Forgave self.

- Recognized that humility gives more power to forgive myself.

HOW TO AVOID FUTURE SLIP-UPS

Here are some common elements that others have used to avoid a slip-up or committing a sin.

- Plan your week emotionally. Try to look ahead and anticipate times when you may be under stress, depressed, or feel self-pity. Deal with your trigger points in advance.

- Avoid becoming overconfident and then forgetting the little things: personal prayer, scripture study, acts of service, etc.

- Avoid living inside your head and not getting outside yourself. Talking to a trusted friend can be very healthy because it helps you to get outside yourself and see things from a different perspective. We spend far too much time living inside of our own heads and not living the fullness of life. Failure to get outside yourself is a major cause for a slip-up.

- Avoid thinking, "It will never happen to me again—I'm beyond that now." Thinking that you are past or beyond a certain point in your recovery and failing to see things as they really are can be the cause of major slip-ups. Be grateful and humble for each day of recovery, but don't be overconfident.

- Avoid thinking, "If only she would do this or if he would do that." The other person may not do anything that you want or need. That's their choice. Realize that you must still find a way to go on even though someone you relied on let you down. Rely only on Christ. He will never let you down.

- Avoid thinking, "I have changed; why hasn't everyone else?" As you see yourself making progress, you may expect others to start changing some of their behaviors. They may or may not decide to change. Focus on yourself. God will give us the power to change ourselves, not others. Try not to let others distract you from your desire to change. If you are not careful, you may find yourself saying, "No one else is changing; why should I?"

- Avoid wanting to change overnight—expecting too much too soon. Change is a process. Be patient. Don't become bored or complacent with the process of recovery. Keep reading, identifying trigger points, and looking for ways to improve each moment and each day.

• One of the best ways to assure yourself of avoiding another slip-up or sin is to make sure you have fully repented of the last slip-up. Fully repenting, in most cases, means that you have discussed it with your bishop and are making daily choices that help you avoid having the problem reoccur. When you do these things, you are blessed with power and strength to assist you in withstanding the temptations of the adversary.

• When you are tempted, don't act immediately on your obsession. Sometimes waiting for two minutes will give you time to divert your attention to something else and get you past the critical point. If you can wait two minutes, you can do it for three minutes. If you can wait three minutes, you can do it for four minutes. Within minutes the obsession will pass and you will be on emotionally stable ground once again.

• Seek friends you can trust, and widen your circle of friends. Someone once said, "A friend is someone who knows all about you and loves you just the same." Trusted friendships make us feel needed, wanted, and accepted. Make every effort to be involved in settings that allow you to meet new friends. Developing a wide circle of trusted friends is emotionally very healthy.

Write some of the choices you can make to avoid a slip-up.

1. _____

_____

2. _____

_____

3. _____

_____

4. _____

_____

5. _____

_____

Perhaps we are much like the pioneers when they became weary of their journey. At times we want to pull over and stop. Perhaps we don't want to try anymore. Perhaps we don't want to go on. Perhaps we have lost hope that we will ever get to Zion. Maybe we don't know of anyone else who has been down the same road and made it to Zion. Perhaps we have seen no victories—only failures. Maybe we have focused on the ruts, the mud, the sand, and the pain. We have seen ourselves deep in the mire. We could not see anyone in sight to help. We felt we were all alone on the prairie of life. Surely the pioneers had those same feelings at times, but the ones we honor *didn't* stop.

The answer is to move on. Take one more step. Look for a different path. There will be time to rest and reflect, but don't dwell on the past. Learn from the past, but don't live in the past. Look forward to the journey. Know that it is a journey. Know that there will still be rocks, boulders, peaks, and valleys. The good news is that the Savior of Mankind can get us through, if we allow Him to do so. He will lift our legs when we are too tired to walk. He will bring us peace when we feel frustrated. He will pull us from the ruts of life and set us back on the course. He will "lead us, guide us, walk beside us, and help us find the way."

No mountain is too tall to climb. No river is too wide to cross. No behavior is so ingrained that the Savior can't remove it. He has all power and will manifest it unto those who seek Him. An unknown author wrote these words:

God Sent Us a Savior
If our greatest need had been information,
God would have sent us an educator.
If our greatest need had been technology,
God would have sent us a scientist.
If our greatest need had been money,
God would have sent us an economist.
But our greatest need was forgiveness,
So God sent us a Savior.

If Christ has the power to move mountains, to feed five thousand with five loaves of bread and two fishes, to heal the sick, to make the blind to see and the lame to walk, He has the power to heal you and me. He has the power to remove our weaknesses if we allow Him. Yes, Jesus is His name. *Turn Yourselves and Live. Is Any Thing Too Hard for the Lord?*

Index

1 Corinthians 13: 4–8, 10
2 Corinthians 7:9–10, 37
1 Nephi 3:7, 114
1 Nephi 15:24, 113
1 Nephi 15:27, 117
3 Nephi 4:33, 42
3 Nephi 9:13, ix, 20, 29
3 Nephi 18:18, 21, 70
2 Nephi 31:20, 23, 142
accept, ix, 16, 19, 24, 28, 40, 46, 57–58, 64, 83, 92, 94, 104–105, 120, 126, 131, 133
addiction, 14–15, 17, 86, 90, 102
admit, 6, 16, 19, 24–25, 36, 133, 150
adversary, 54, 112–113, 137, 158
affair, 88, 90
affection, 47, 89, 95
Alma 7:15, 104
Alma 22:15, 100, 101
Alma 22:18, 101
Alma 24:10, 20, 33
Alma 31:10, 110
Alma 33:11, 111
Alma 37:33, viii, 21, 98
Alma 42:30, 19, 24–25
anger, 2–3, 18, 74–75, 86, 90–91, 94, 96, 103, 116, 121, 129, 132–134
appetite(s), 9, 71, 140
Ashton, Marvin J., 43
Atonement, x, 28, 31, 82, 84, 144, 155
Ballard, Russell M., 115
behavior, viii, 5–9, 12–13, 15–21, 24, 37–38, 43, 45–48 , 50, 53, 57, 65, 70, 73–75, 82–83, 85, 90–91, 93–96, 98–99, 101–102, 106, 119, 124, 128, 135, 143, 154–155, 160
believe, 9–10, 38, 82, 85, 87, 91–92, 120, 142, 145–148
Benson, Ezra Taft, 36, 38, 100, 111, 130–131, 134, 144, 149
bishop, 8, 18, 25, 38–40, 49, 52–53, 57, 88, 119, 125, 132, 158
Book of Mormon, 41, 143, 149, 151–152
boredom, 75
boundaries, 9, 91, 96
broken heart & contrite spirit, 36–37, 57, 132
Burton, Theodore M., 35, 39, 41, 142
Cannon, George Q., 116
charity, 10, 81, 85
Charlotte's Web, 76–77
child molestation, 9
Christ, viii, ix, x, 5, 7, 14, 16–17, 19–24, 28–32, 35, 37, 38, 40, 46, 49, 51–52,
54–56, 62–63, 74–76, 79, 81–82, 84–85, 95, 98, 100–101, 107–108, 110, 112, 114, 120, 122, 128, 130–137, 142, 144–146, 152–157, 160
Christ–centered Rational Thoughts, 20, 43–45, 47, 49, 51, 53, 55, 57, 59, 61, 63, 65, 68
church disciplinary system, 13
Church, 13, 38, 40, 46, 56–57, 59–60, 79–81, 84–85, 88, 100, 110–111, 122, 125, 152–154
compulsive behavior pattern, 6, 15, 82, 93
compulsive sexual lifestyle, viii
computer chat lines, 103
computer pornography, 103
confessing (ion), 25, 38–40, 49, 132
consecration, 100
converted, ix, 20, 29
counselor, vii, 8, 81
covenants, 40, 58, 81, 84, 116, 152
D&C 23:1, 98
D&C 38:14, 138
D&C 61:2, 97
D&C 64:9–10, 41
D&C 84:88, 138
D&C 88:63, 138
D&C 88:119–120, 22, 139
D&C 88:126, 138
darkness, 40, 42, 49, 116
deny (ied), (ial), 6, 13, 16, 19, 24–25, 27, 79, 83, 86, 94
depressed (ion), 1, 4–5, 87, 90–91, 96, 115–116, 147, 156
despair, 2, 9, 35, 143–144
devil, viii, 21, 78, 98, 108
disciplinary council, 13
discouragement, 9, 144, 150
Divine Nature, 136
doubt, 2, 116
drug, viii, 8–9, 17, 63, 65, 70, 72, 75, 85, 129
drug of lust, 8–9, 17, 70, 72, 85, 129
dysfunctional family, 86
ecclesiastical leaders, 15
emotional out–of–balance behaviors, viii
emotions, viii, 6, 8, 15, 17–18, 21, 30, 53, 55, 70, 73–75, 77, 83, 94, 98–100, 109, 111–112, 118, 121, 125–126, 133, 137
endure to the end, 23, 41, 142
Enos 1:5, 138
Ensign, ix, 9, 35, 37, 39, 41, 44, 99, 100, 101, 110, 111, 115, 116, 130, 131, 134, 143, 144–145, 149, 152

Ether 12:27, 22, 128, 130–131
excommunicated, 80, 83
exercise, 22, 56, 139–141
exhibitionism, 9
failure, 9, 156
faith, viii, 2, 21–22, 33, 54, 88, 92, 95, 98,
    101, 130–133, 139, 146–148, 150,
    154–155
fantasy (s), (sized), (sizing), 4, 12–15, 58,
    80, 83, 89, 120
fast, 22, 81, 139, 148
fear, 2, 89, 91, 96, 104, 150
feelings, vii, 3, 6, 8–9, 12, 15, 17–18, 27,
    36, 48, 53, 55, 57, 62, 71, 73, 75, 83,
    85–86, 88, 91, 94, 96, 99, 103, 106,
    115, 118, 120–121, 125, 134, 140, 159
filthiness, 117
forgiven (ness), 9, 20, 33, 39, 41, 59, 81,
    84, 86, 137–138, 160
foundation, ix, 7, 21–22, 33, 38, 108–109
free agency, 74, 100
Friend's Story, 11, 78, 85
frustration, 9, 75, 80, 83, 115, 150
Garden of Gethsemane, 125
gay, 26, 65
God, ix, 6, 8–9, 19–25, 29–31, 33, 35–38,
    41–49, 51, 54–56, 58–59, 62, 64–65,
    69, 74, 76, 78–79, 85, 92, 99–101, 104,
    106, 108–111, 113, 115–116, 120, 122,
    125–126, 128–130, 133–137, 139,
    141–143, 146–148, 153, 155, 157, 160
Godly sorrow, 36–37, 122, 136
gospel, vii, 14, 17, 100, 146, 151–152, 154
grace, 22, 34, 82, 130–133
grain bin, 2–8, 17, 74, 102
group program (therapy), 87, 92, 95
guilty, 1, 3–4, 46, 55, 122
happiness, 36, 57, 82, 86, 96
heal (ed), (ing), vii, 20, 29–31, 40,
    112–114, 130, 160
heal weaknesses, ix, 130
Heavenly Father, 5, 21, 31, 35, 38, 41, 47,
    55, 60, 63–64, 88, 92–93, 95–96,
    98–100, 106–108, 110–111, 115, 121,
    126, 133, 143
Helaman 4:26, 112
Helaman 5:12, ix, x, 22, 108
heterosexual relationships, 9
Hinckley, Gordon B., 44
Holy Ghost, 41, 51, 131, 146
homosexual, 9, 26
hope, 2, 10–11, 15, 19, 23, 30, 40, 57, 142,
    144–145, 159
hopelessness, 9
humble (humility) viii, 8, 21–22, 31, 33,
    34, 40, 42, 53, 97–98, 101, 106, 126,
    130–133, 155–156, 157
hymns, 113, 129
immorality, 37
inappropriate sexual behavior, 19, 24
incest, 9
Internet, 54, 103

intimacy, 89–90
irrational thinking patterns, viii
irritable, 1, 10
Is Any Thing Too Hard for the Lord?, 2, 160
isolation, 6–7, 16, 38, 83, 95
Jesus Christ, viii, 20–21, 29, 31, 37, 46, 55,
    81, 98, 108, 114, 120, 136, 146,
    152–156
John 5:8, 97
John 5:39, 97
John 6:20, 97
John 8:7, 97
John 8:31–32, 97
John 10:14, 97
John 12:46, 138
John 14:27, x
journal, 55, 143
Journal of Discourses, 10:173, 137
joy, 35, 41, 82, 100–101, 106, 111
Keep the Commandments, 14, 17, 41
Kimball, Spencer W., 33–34, 75, 154
Lamb, 2–7, 74, 102, 153
Lee, Harold B., 110–111
Lehi, 117
lesbian, 9, 27
light, 40, 42, 49, 70, 93, 96, 106, 107, 113,
    138
light of Christ, 40, 107
life (live), 2, 5, 8, 12, 14–16, 28, 30, 38,
    42, 54, 60, 72, 74, 76, 80, 82, 84, 86,
    87, 92, 94, 96, 100, 102, 106, 112, 114,
    131–132, 134, 136, 137, 144, 146,
    152, 154–156, 159–160,
lonely (liness), 2, 4, 6, 9, 18, 71, 75–76, 86,
    94, 99, 109
Lord, viii, 2, 10–11, 14–15, 17–19, 21–22,
    29–31, 34–36, 38, 40–42, 44, 56, 58,
    81, 84, 86, 97–98, 100, 113–114, 116,
    131, 137, 139, 143–144, 146, 160
love, 2, 9–10, 14, 19, 22–23, 28, 31, 38,
    47–49, 51, 57–59, 61, 77, 81, 92,
    96–97, 99, 106, 110–111, 114–115,
    118, 120, 125, 129–130, 136, 142
low self–esteem, 9, 75, 87, 98
lust, 8–12, 15–17, 51, 58, 65, 70–72, 85,
    129, 155
lustful thoughts, 11, 47
mantle, 40, 49
Mark 9:25–29, 141
marriage, vii, 10, 12, 15, 45, 47, 51, 58–61,
    80, 83, 88–90, 94, 103, 152
masturbation, 9, 11–12, 15–16, 26, 47, 55,
    80, 83
Matthew 7:7, 32
Matthew 7:8, 97
Maxwell, Neal A., 70–71, 99–100
merciful, 35, 97, 138, 143
mercy, 41, 113–114, 132, 143
miracle, 33, 129, 134
mistake, 64, 156
Monson, Thomas S., 111
Mormon 2:13–14, 36

Mormon 5:2, 30, 99
Mormon 5:16, 29
Mormon 5:17, 31
Mormon 5:18, 31–32
Mormon 9:31, 20, 43
Mosiah 2:17, 41, 143
Mosiah 3:19, 31
Mosiah 4:27, 115
necking, 11
Nephi, ix, 20–21, 23, 29, 42, 70, 113–114, 117, 142
Oaks, Dallin H., 115
obedience, 50
obsession, 14, 17, 49, 65, 158
out of balance emotions, 100, 111
overconfident, 156
pain (ful), 8, 14–15, 17, 35, 62–63, 89–90, 93, 96, 102, 125, 143, 146–147, 150, 159
Parable of the Smiling Pumpkin, 104–107
Parable of the Lamb, 2–5, 6, 102
parents, vii, 2–3, 6–7, 26, 39, 57, 79, 87, 115–116, 133, 136
passions, 140
patience, 92, 96, 147, 149–150
peace, ix, x, 2, 20, 29, 38, 42, 82, 97, 102, 118, 128–129, 145, 160
petting, 11
physical exercise, 22, 139
piano lessons, 123
pioneers, 159
pleasure, 6, 12, 26
poems, 150, 160
pornography, 9, 47, 54, 79–80, 82, 103, 119
pray (er), 21–22, 30, 33–34, 48, 63–64, 70, 81, 84, 92, 98–99, 101, 106, 109–113, 115, 121, 129, 133, 139–141, 155–156
premarital sex, 11
pride, 20, 33, 38–39, 49, 52–53, 98, 103
priesthood leaders, 81
procreation, 125
Progressive Steps, 134, 146, 151, 154
promises, 14, 17, 40, 131
promptings, 111
prophets, 11, 36, 50, 54, 57, 137
prostitution, 9
psychologist, 87
rational thoughts, 20, 43, 68
rationalization (ized), 7, 25, 27–28, 44
recovery, viii, ix, x, 2, 15, 19, 24–25, 38, 86, 154, 157, 164
rejected, 2, 4, 53, 73, 106, 118
remorse, 12, 15, 36
repentance, viii, 14–15, 17, 20–21, 33–39, 42, 48–50, 56–57, 81, 98, 137, 143–144, 146, 154–156
restitution, 39–40, 59
Restoration, 151
romantic intrigue, 90, 94
Romney, Marion G., 110
Satan, 9–10, 13–14, 21, 25, 31, 38, 40, 49, 54, 59, 65, 70, 74, 115–116, 123, 125, 137, 143–144

Savior, ix, x, 5, 14, 17, 35, 37, 56–57, 63, 97, 100, 102, 125, 128–129, 137–138, 142, 149, 160
Scott, Richard G., 9
scriptures. see 1 Cor. 5:1, 3 Ne. 9:20; Moro. 6:2; D&C 20:37, 59:8; Ps. 34:18, 57:17; Isa. 57:15, 37
self–deceit, 44
self–gratification, 9
self–hatred, 91–92, 94, 96
self–mastery, 44
self–pity, 2–4, 6, 74–75, 156
selfishness, 70, 103
sex, vii, 10–13, 26–27, 43, 45, 47, 49–51, 53, 59–61, 75, 87, 89, 95, 101, 103, 118, 124
sex perversion, 11
sex addict, 11, 13
sexual relations, 10, 12, 15, 47, 61, 103
sexual obsessions, 48
shame, 55, 88
sin, 12, 36–37, 39–41, 47, 50, 87, 97, 99–100, 104, 123, 132, 137, 144, 156, 158
Smith, Joseph, 78, 152–153
sobriety, 14, 155
sorrow, 35–37, 63, 122, 136, 143
spiritual surgery, ix
spouse, 25–26, 39, 53, 57, 61, 102, 106, 115, 131, 151
Step One, 19, 24
Step Two, 20, 29
Step Three, 20, 33
Step Four, 20, 43
Step Five, 21, 70
Step Six, 21, 98
Step Seven, 21, 108
Step Eight, 22, 130
Step Nine, 22, 139
Step Ten, 23, 142
steps of repentance, 20, 33–42, 50, 56–57, 137
strengths, 22, 49, 58, 130, 132
stress, 25, 36, 74–75, 119, 140, 156
success, x, 6, 34, 75, 134, 147
support group, viii, 13, 18, 125
suppress, 48, 80
surrender (ed), (ing), ix, x, 5–7, 11, 14, 16–19, 21, 37, 48, 55, 63, 65, 74, 76, 79, 84–85, 95, 98–105, 111–112, 126, 128–129, 132–135, 137, 143–144
Temple, 12, 45, 58, 111, 141, 149, 154
tempt (tation), viii, 7, 14, 21, 59, 70, 88, 98, 110, 137
Ten–step program, x
tension, 140
testimony, vii, 86
The Grain Bin, 2–8, 17, 74, 102
The Ten Steps, 19, 78, 145
thoughts, 2, 11, 13, 20, 27, 30, 43–45, 47–48, 58, 68, 75, 80, 99–100, 114, 118, 121–122, 124–125, 140

transgression (s), 18, 39, 50, 59, 80, 84,
     112, 123
trigger points, 17, 21, 70–79, 85, 98, 108,
     115, 117, 118–128, 155–157
trusted, 7–8, 18, 106, 109, 156, 158
trusted friend, 8, 106, 109, 156
twelve–step support group, 13
unassigned service, 109, 115–116
unconditional love, 19, 28, 97, 125
unresolved feelings, 6, 15, 83, 94
unseen wounds, 113–114
unwanted Feelings, 17, 75
victory, x, 12, 100, 134
voyeurism, 9
weakness (es), viii, 11, 22, 49, 58, 60, 81,
     84, 130, 132–134, 149, 151, 160
Where Can I Turn for Peace?, 129
wholesome sex, 10, 47
women, 12–13, 15–16, 36, 56, 58–59, 90,
     123–126
worldly sorrow, 36, 136
worthlessness, 9
Young, Brigham, 137